Surviving Saturn's Return

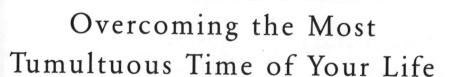
Overcoming the Most Tumultuous Time of Your Life

SHERENE SCHOSTAK, M.A.
AND STEFANIE IRIS WEISS, M.A.

Contemporary Books

Chicago   New York   San Francisco   Lisbon   London   Madrid   Mexico City
Milan   New Delhi   San Juan   Seoul   Singapore   Sydney   Toronto

Library of Congress Cataloging-in-Publication Data

Schostak, Sherene.
     Surviving saturn's return : overcoming the most tumultuous time of your life /
Sherene Schostak, Stefanie Iris Weiss. — 1st ed.
          p.   cm.
     ISBN 0-07-142196-3 (pbk. : alk. paper)
          1. Human beings—Effect of Saturn on.   2. Astrology.   I. Weiss, Stefanie Iris.
II. Title.

     BF1724.2.S3S36   2004
     133.5'37'08422—dc22   2003014508

1 2 3 4 5 6 7 8 9 0   AGM/AGM   2 1 0 9 8 7 6 5 4 3

ISBN 0-07-142196-3

Interior design by Steve Straus

For Amma,
the true inspiration for our work—may healing flow
into all those that read this book
through her loving, divine spirit.

Contents

Acknowledgments

From my heart I want to express my love and appreciation

To my rock of Gibraltar, my real-life Saturn father, Phillip H. Schostak; my mystical, belly-dancing, goddess mommy, Lise Schostak; and my beloved Jupiter angel Gad Cohen; with much gratitude and respect to my Ashtanga teacher, Eddie Stern, for cracking me up through my relentless battle with the Marichasanas

To my childhood friend of twenty-five years, Kerry Johnston

To my sexy Scorpio sister and fabulous travel companion, Dom, who is always there for me

To all of the lovely and talented Zodiac Dancers and crew

To my business partner and amazing friend, Tet, who brought Zodiac Dance to life

To my beautiful friends Liza, Neena, Zack, Elissa, Wendy, Elysha, and Nahja

To my cousin, Jerry Schostak, for his generosity and support of my studies at the New School

To my incredible clients, who are my real teachers

To my astrology mentors, Edwin Steinbrecher and Stephen Connors of D.O.M.E.

—Sherene Schostak

I owe profound gratitude to a generous assortment of compassionate cohorts—those who have undertaken this journey with me. Endless love and thanks to my wonderful family—my beautiful Libra mom, my forever tinkering Aquarius dad, and my brilliant Virgo brother, Hal. Eternal props to my magnificent and matchless troupe of friends: Liz, Jodi, Ora, Rachelle, Peter, Henry, Missy, PJ, Monica, Lynn, Jaimie, Noel, Talya, Dom, Gabby, and Josh.

Extra cuddles to my animal companions for love and appropriately timed licks: Boodle, Roxy, and Rufus.

Many thanks to each of my writing and gender studies students, for teaching me almost everything I know.

—Stefanie Iris Weiss

Finally, both Sherene and Stefanie would like to thank Jennifer Unter, their fabulous agent, for guiding them through the treacherous waters of birthing a book.

And, as classic Saturn in Taurus women, we have to thank all of the New York restaurants that provided the croissants, cappuccinos, many glasses of Cotes Du Rhone, and every variety of chocolate dessert that made this book possible, especially Bar Pitti, Pastis, Balthazar, Joe's, Doma, Ino, and Otto.

Introduction

It often comes as news to women that one does not die when one turns thirty. Many women in their late twenties live in sheer, unadulterated fear of the big three-oh. Sometimes we discuss it openly, and sometimes we keep it a shameful secret. The truth is that even the most enlightened woman making the transition to thirty lives with a fair amount of pure panic.

It's not our fault. Our society is focused mercilessly on youth, beauty, companionship, and fertility. We're supposed to own each of these in equal measure. And we're not supposed to sweat it. It's a tough job, even for those of us who are perfectly endowed with all of the above. For those of us who lack these graces, the daily struggles are far more formidable. It ain't easy, ladies.

The lens of the world has been aimed lately on the lot of us. Women in their thirties are under the microscope right now. Even if we don't possess perfectly flat tummies, Prada bags, and knights in shining armor, our stories are finally being told. Maybe you are past the days of wanting to join MTV on spring break but aren't quite ready to settle into a quiet, suburban life. Or maybe you do enjoy a quiet lifestyle but know that life is really just beginning. Maybe you share cocktails with girlfriends and live the single life. Maybe you have a husband. Maybe your partner is a woman. You might be a high-powered executive or a stay-at-home mom. Whoever or wherever you are, if you are around the age of twenty-five to thirty-five, you are likely being spun around like Dorothy in the proverbial twister of life: you are in the prime of your first Saturn Return (SR). Turning thirty doesn't suck simply because society says so. There is science behind the suffering.

Why Astrology Works

Read this section only if you question the validity of astrology. Even if you're not the type to indulge in tarot readings, to believe in psychic phenomena, or to sage your apartment to remove old spirits, we think that astrology might just become one of the most-often-used instruments in your toolbox. Lest you assume that astrology eliminates the power of free will, we aim to show you just the opposite. Astrology lays out the possibilities so that you can have a road map instead of mindlessly refusing to ask for directions.

In brief, we offer this defense of astrology to skeptics. If you're familiar with only newspaper horoscopes, you might think astrology is complete nonsense, or worse. But on any full moon try checking with your local psychiatric ward, visiting a police precinct, or talking to a doctor about the events that unfold in emergency rooms. Stories of strange behavior and havoc abound. All of this hints at just how much celestial bodies can affect us deep in our own bodies and minds. Scientists have long known that the moon has a gravitational pull on the movement of the tides. How can we, as nature's creatures, not feel the pull of the planets?

We need to answer our skeptics (and we know there are many of them). We don't expect you to believe in astrology just because we tell you to. Think about it like this: astrophysics works within the rubric of speculative theory, as does astrology. Just because we work theoretically does not imply that our theories will eventually be refuted. Currently accepted science, as it stands, has not yet found the "proof" we seek, the hard science that says that cosmic bodies do absolutely influence our psyches and our everyday lives. The proof we *do* have is in the data: since the Chinese and Babylonians began their studies of the movements of the planets thousands of years ago, to the development of Western astrology (when astrology and astronomy were considered twin sciences), to the harder computer-based information collected in the last half of the past century, there is a vast bank of astrological scholarship to mine.

Carl Sagan, world-renowned scientist, said of astrology, "That we can think of no mechanism for astrology is relevant, but unconvincing. No mechanism was known, for example, for continental drift when it was proposed by Wegener. Nevertheless, we see that Wegener was right, and those who objected on the grounds of unavailable mechanism were wrong." Maybe we don't know yet exactly *why* the planets' energies affect us, but one thing we know is that they *do*, indeed, affect us. Robert Hand, one of the premier astrological scholars, says, "We should not be trying to explain astrology by means of science as it is, but there is no problem with trying to explain astrology by a science that has not yet come to be."

Physics 101

Since Einstein offered us the theory of relativity, the old paradigm of enlightenment science—the old-school cause-and-effect proof—has not meant what it once did. But somehow we Westerners are still caught up in this worldview. This is frustrating to metaphysicians and even modern physicists, whose aim is to get a grip on the broader scope of the universe that we inhabit. Werner Heisenberg's Uncertainty Principle showed that cause and effect is not actually measurable because the order of events depends on our location in the space-time continuum. Quantum physics seeks to show us the fourth dimension. We can't see it with our eyes, at least not yet, but it's still considered a valid enterprise, one which billions of dollars are poured into on a consistent basis. (Chaos theory, nonlinear dynamics, and fractal geometry are a few areas of interest for those intrigued by the intersection between astrology and science.)

Astrophysicists tell us that the stuff of our bodies comes from supernova explosions, stellar evolution, and the formation of our solar system. Solar storms have a powerful effect on radio broadcasts and seem to have an effect on the weather as well. Approximately 10^{10} neutrinos per second are going through each square centimeter of our heads every moment. We are continuously swathed in streams of radiation from outer space. Comets and asteroids that crashed into the earth in the geologic past have markedly affected biological history and, therefore, our evolution—our very bodies and minds. Watching friends and clients curl up like the toes of the Wicked Witch of the West under the brick house of the Saturn Return has shown us that we're not taking much of a leap when we say the planets play a part in the great dramas that unfold in our lives. (If you're a hardheaded skeptic and need more information, check out the references in the last section of the book, "Additional Reading.")

Psychology 101

Only in the last century have millions of willing subjects put their hearts and minds in the hands of psychotherapists, whose science is considered soft. Sigmund Freud, Carl Jung, and Alfred Adler created a system of the psyche that is valued world-over, constantly updated and built upon, and still a multimillion dollar industry. Yet there is little in the way of "hard" science to prove its value. It is accepted, though, and vaunted by the best of the academic lot. Why is astrology still relegated to the margins? Still considered entertainment? Much of contemporary astrology (the kind we practice, FYI) is linked to psychotherapy, and to Jung's theories of synchronicity, personality type, and individuation. Ever notice those freaky little moments when you're thinking about a song and it comes on the radio, or your friend calls the moment you conjure her image in your mind? Or why three people have uncannily similar experiences and tell you about them on the same day? You may call these idiosyncrasies random coincidence if you like, or you can call upon the principle of synchronicity to help you figure out why you're being called to attention at these moments. These are *meaningful* coincidences and astrology works on this level as well. Saturn tells us that every encounter, every moment, is a lesson.

Women and Power

Our most beloved teacher/guru, Mata Amritanandamayi, offers the following women's wisdom:

Antiquated, crippling concepts devised in the past are blocking women from reaching spiritual heights. Those are the shadows that still haunt women, evoking fear and distrust within. Women should let go of their fear and distrust, they are simply illusions. The limitations women think they have are not real. Women need to muster the strength to overcome those imagined limitations. They already possess this power; it is right here! And once that power has been evoked, no one will be able to stop the forward march of women in every area of life.

—From *Immortal Bliss* (vol. 16, no. 2)

We offer this book as a tool for all women bearing their many crosses, because we know (from experience) that it's easier than you think.

What the Hell Is the Saturn Return, Anyway?

Perhaps you've picked up this book because you've heard the term "Saturn Return" bandied about lately. Michael Stipe, lead singer of REM, wrote a song about it a few years ago. So did Gwen Stefani from No Doubt, right before she turned thirty. Maybe you're reading this simply because you are in your late twenties or early thirties and are desperately in search of an anchor. Take heart. You are not alone. Any floating feelings of anxiety or world-weariness that you may be carrying are totally normal now. Astrologers have known about this powerful phenomenon for years, and now it's time for you to get on board and grab some comfort. This is how it works, in brief. Starting at around age twenty-seven, something profound happens to us. We are transformed. (Please note that one can begin to feel the effects of the Saturn Return several years prior to the twenty-seventh birthday, and the reverberations can last into the mid-thirties.) It is often a time of chaos, constriction, and confusion that can end in catharsis. Sound familiar? If you haven't yet reached this milestone, do a quick survey of your friends that have borne witness and made it into their early thirties. Your assessment will likely reveal stories of deep crisis, fear, depression, and turmoil. (If you've picked up this book because you're just hitting this age bracket or if you're already in the throes of it, you probably know what we're talking about.) This journey does not take place because we have come to the base of the mountain openly seeking salvation. Most of us go kicking and screaming. Who looks forward to turning thirty? (If you raised your hand, you are a rare breed, dear.) The change is unavoidable, profoundly personal, and often earth-shattering. Astrologers (at work on this issue for five thousand years, at least) know that when Saturn returns to its original location in the birth chart, a revolution takes place. Saturn is known as the bringer of life's most important lessons. He wakes us up. (We'll learn more about Saturn shortly. Please note that we refer to him in the masculine because he is symbolic of the father.) At the time of the Saturn Return, we leave things behind and start over. This is the precipice of adulthood. Now childhood is finally and irrevocably over. The transformation doesn't happen when we turn twenty-one, when we graduate college, or when we face any of the innumerable milestones of early adult life. The Saturn Return ushers us into real adult life, finally and forever. We have a choice at this moment, and if we make the right decision and live out the will of our hearts, the next twenty-nine and a half years (the time it takes to get to the next Saturn Return) will be richer, happier, and smoother.

Here is the simple science behind the experience. Each planet moves through the zodiac at a different rate of speed. The sun spends just about a month in each sign. If you were born between March 20 and April 20, approximately, you are an Aries. And so on. This is simply your sun sign, what you tell people when they ask, "What's your sign?" But your chart is far more complicated than that. Your natal chart is like a photograph of the heavens above you the moment you were born. It is your astrological map. Akin to a fingerprint, or better yet a psychic blueprint, it can show who you are, who you've been, and who you might become. Everyone's chart is completely unique. In it sit the planets: Mercury, Venus, Mars, Jupiter, and so on. Astrologers look at the sun and moon (referred to as the *lights*) and eight different planets when they cast your chart. Each relates to some aspect of your life. Just like all the other planets of the solar system, Saturn moves in its orbit around the sun, taking some time to explore each of the twelve signs. Saturn spends about two and a half years in each sign of the zodiac. This means that when you were born, Saturn was sitting somewhere in the sky, and therefore in your chart—in Taurus, Gemini, Cancer, and so on, depending on the time and place of your birth. This is how we figure out what sector of your life Saturn pitched camp in when you arrived on earth. Wherever he decided to park his hearse is the area of life that you'll find laden with his lessons. When you look at Figure 1, you'll see that every slice of the pie covers major issues for women—self-esteem, food, sexuality, relationships, and so on. Wherever he came a callin' when you were born is exactly where he intends to make you do your work. And when he comes back around to this same spot at the Saturn Return, things get complicated and crisis generally ensues around those very issues. Later in this chapter we'll show you exactly how to find out where Saturn lives in your own personal chart. He is the one that represents your challenges, and he is the utmost location scout. He knows your karma. He will choose the proper real estate in your birth chart, and this choice will be a running theme throughout your life. The motif Saturn has chosen for you will likely resonate in all of your experience, sometimes like a frustratingly bad, scratched record stuck on repeat. At the Saturn Return, you can carefully lift the needle and place it back in its cradle. This is your chance to choose your own theme music. We'll get to all of this in more detail a bit later. First, let's meet His High Darkness, Lord Saturn.

Who Is Saturn?

Saturn is the most maligned of all the planets. People have feared him from time immemorial. He is known as the Lord of Karma, the taskmaster, and Father Time. His awful gaze in Indian mythology has been known to turn other deities' heads to ashes and curse even the greatest of the gods with just a glance. Saturn is considered to be the most challenging planet. Mythology and astrology both support this. (Many ancient cultures, from Greco-Roman to Hindu, have presented

Saturn as a mean, cruel guy. And astrologers know that he's a ball breaker because of their clients' stories. We'll let you in on some harrowing Saturn tales as we progress.)

Saturn is perhaps the guru of all gurus, which in Sanskrit translates as the great teacher who removes (*ru*) the darkness (*gu*). This is why

FIGURE 1   The twelve lessons of Saturn

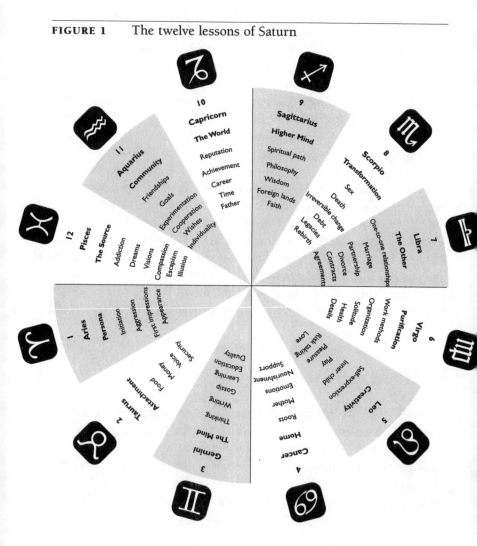

Saturn is classically linked with depression, fear, and darkness. In order to remove the darkness, he will first exaggerate it to make damn sure you hit rock bottom, just so you can come out on the other side. This is one of the reasons Saturn's location in your birth chart makes you feel inferior in that area of your life. Saturn tends to create this darkness only to make you see the light. The Saturn Return presents you with an opportunity to get in touch with your karma, to duel with it, and to win accolades when you're done. But there is absolutely no sidestepping with the great cosmic taskmaster. You may have read about gurus in India initiating their disciples by forcing them to stand on one leg for days, or fast for a month. It often feels like you are undergoing such austerity when facing a Saturn initiation, especially if you have not been doing your inner work. The Saturn Return is his signature initiation. If you can pass his hardest trial, you can probably ace the rest of his exams throughout your life.

The gravity of Saturn work cannot be emphasized enough. Saturn shows us that the only way to freedom is through self-possession. This is why he is the great teacher: because he doesn't merely feed us, he teaches us how to fish. He invites us to finally meet our true self—not hypothetically or theoretically, but in living color and in the present, perfect moment. The fear, difficulty, and depression often connected with Saturn are in proportion to the degree that we refuse to own the authority in our lives. How long are we going to remain dependent children to our parents, or Mother Church, or our alma mater? Do we let them set the rules and decide our worth, our values, our structure, and our fate? Or do we do the deep, dark soul work—mine all of the unknowns in the depths of our solitude, where we might glimpse some glint of uncontaminated spirit in our core? Saturn teaches us to take care of ourselves and to please ourselves instead of merely being good little girls forever. In the hero adventure, made famous by Joseph Campbell, the hero has to travel into the darkest uncharted regions and face every inner demon, obstacle, crisis, and outcast complex imaginable. In order for the hero to come out on the other side, he or she must surrender to the metaphorical belly of the whale in order to return totally transformed for the freedom and good of his or her people.

Soon after the tragic terrorist attacks in New York on September 11, 2001, we recognized an unsettling but profound connection. The World Trade Center, believe it or not, was in its first Saturn Return when it was destroyed. The twin towers were finished in 1973, when Saturn was last in Gemini, sign of the twins. The towers were twenty-eight years old when they went down. And this unbelievably literal metaphor is useful for us: when we are in our Saturn Return, we often feel like the building of our soul is collapsing. It is a time to tear down the old structures that are no longer supporting us and to begin anew. If we don't let go of that which fails to fortify our true potential but rather imprisons us in a false tower, Saturn will come to drag us back to the ground.

Saturn and the Real World: What Does the Saturn Return Really Feel Like?

If you're about to hit your Saturn Return, you may be in a state of complete crisis. Everyone's Saturn Return is different, but there are some common issues that all of those close to thirty deal with. You may feel isolated and afraid, question all of your decisions, have crying fits, break off relationships (or start profound new ones), quit your job, feel like a failure, decide that what you've been doing with your life for the past X number of years has been total BS, feel more neurotic than you ever have in your life, have a mini (or maybe a major) mental breakdown, hate your parents and other authority figures, and generally wonder who the hell you are. This is just the tip of the iceberg. But remember, Saturn offers us a solution even as he puts us through life's meat grinder. There is a method to his madness. (We'll say this ad nauseam, so much so that you may get really pissed off.)

Let us offer a few brief examples. One of the first women we interviewed when we started research on this book illustrates a classic Saturn Return scenario. We first met Andrea when she was twenty-seven.

She was in a long-term relationship and had been unhappy in it for almost a year, but she clung to it for security because she feared being alone. This was particularly true because as she approached her Saturn Return, her life felt like chaos. She felt like rugs were being pulled out from under her wherever she went. Just as she hit the prime of her Saturn Return, her reliable boyfriend suddenly broke up with her, sending her into shock. Although she knew he was holding her back from life experience, she went into severe depression and mourned for him for months. When she finally came out of her depression, she felt totally liberated and realized that the breakup was probably the best thing that ever happened to her. It was a trial by fire, but now she was cleansed and ready to start her life again. When we met with her again a few years later, she was self-possessed, confident, and making her own rules. This was something no one could ever take away from her.

Sarah was already in the throes of her Saturn Return when we met her at the age of twenty-nine. She was miserable in her job, a paper-pushing, go-nowhere career that had never fulfilled her. She questioned everything she'd been doing in the past seven years. But she was afraid to leave the job because of the security it offered: health care, a pension, and a regular paycheck. What she really wanted was to be a writer. She took a chance and quit, without building up her savings beforehand. She found herself having to do some serious bootstraps work, living on pennies, and facing a drastic change in lifestyle. But she was so glad that she took the risk. Although she suffered through some months of fear, in the end she came out on top. Article by article, she created a freelance life for herself and now, at thirty-two, has carved out a place for herself at a top magazine. She overcame her fear. Her work now reflects her values, and she loves waking up in the morning and getting down to business.

Saturn and Solitude

Saturn will bring you to the edge of solitude and wall you in, isolate you, and exclude you from the outer world if that is what it takes to do his work. He will not let you get away with letting other people do the work for you. This is what it really means to come into your own and to grow up (a few of Saturn's campaign promises). To the degree we consciously or unconsciously elicit other people to snap us into shape, set the rules, pat us on the back, or set the boundaries, he will surely sentence us to profound exile. Saturn's work is done in solitude, which is why he is often depicted as a hermit. To get our attention, he may in some way separate us from our greatest protection against the cold: our loved ones. This is all to bring us to that which sustains us at our very core when all external forms of support are not there. He is an ally in that his vision for us is nothing less than that of a great father. Put simply, he wants us to manifest our potential, accomplish our dreams, be indebted to no one, and be true to ourselves. He can't bear to see our dreams or our potential unrealized, going nowhere. He wants us to finally get done what we proclaim with every New Year's resolution. (Interestingly, New Year's Day falls when the sun is in Saturn's sign, Capricorn.) He asks us how we can bring the material and the spiritual together within us. Saturn guards the threshold between the two worlds, standing in the doorway between the personal and the collective both in the solar system and in our psyches.

Saturn, Authority, and Time

Saturn symbolizes our earliest encounters with authority. For women, Saturn is the first run-in with our fathers, setting the stage for how we will see and interact with men in our life. Saturn teaches us to stop seeking the father's approval. This can come in many guises, depending on who plays father for us. Saturn is also connected to discipline, responsibility, tradition, contraction, conventionality, old age, teachers, reality, ambition, accomplishment, and self-reliance. The old, wise, ringed one stands alone symbolically among the rest of the planets. He is not pretty or sweet, like Venus. He's not dreamy or misty, like Neptune. In fact, Saturn is the big clock inside of us. He tells us what time it is. Saturn is a planet of the now, not later. No other teacher will so ruthlessly show us the value of every grain of sand in the hourglass and drive home the slogan: "There is no time like the present." Deadlines are ruled by Saturn. When you miss one, the guilt you feel is his slap, his thunderclap. He rules lead, the heaviest of elements. How much weight do all of our unfinished tasks or neglected responsibilities carry? Especially at the Saturn Return, if we don't address those lessons that our cosmic daddy has been patiently yet consistently trying to alert us to, he can show up in our life as a seemingly externally imposed crisis. Maybe as a stiff spine or another physical problem, a dental problem (he also rules our teeth and bones), a problem with authority figures, or issues with our father. Wherever the deficits were in your experience of father is where Saturn will use life and experience to reparent you based on these earlier gaps. Teachers, older friends, and boyfriends may stand in for Dad before the Saturn Return to heal what was missing. For better or worse, at the Saturn Return, Dad has to be found on the inside. Even if yours was a superstar hero dad, Saturn will force you to let go and depend on the inner version.

Learning to Use the Force

Why are we telling you to bow down to such a meanie? Because the truth is, Saturn is the only planet in the solar system that teaches you who you really are by telling you who you aren't. He won't let you get away with lying to yourself. If you're not being brutally honest with yourself in every way, Saturn is apt to set up circumstances to make you face your dishonesty. If you are hiding out in a dead relationship, or a job that doesn't feed you in the way that you need to be fed, or if you're finding some other way to suppress your karmic reality, Saturn will wait patiently, at first, for you to rise to the occasion. If you refuse, he'll light the fuse attached to the firecracker of your life and wait, again, for you to smell the flame. If you inhale deeply and proceed to don your favorite pair of denial-style nose plugs, he will likely ignite an explosion under your ass. It will hurt, and then you'll get it. He wants you to get it, of course, before it gets this far gone.

Wherever Saturn shows up in the birth chart, a lack is felt to show the opportunities that lie beneath it. There is gold underneath your tar, an alchemical miracle at the center of any painful crucible you find yourself in. When Saturn compresses you, he does so to show you what you're made of. If Saturn's position in your chart says that you have issues with blocked creativity, he will not let you waste your masterpiece potential. If his lesson concerns painful relationships, then meeting his karmic challenge is likely to bring you the highest level of relationship potential in a true marriage of equals. The hardship, with Saturn, can turn into a kind of earthly paradise, if you learn to listen to him right. Saturn is in charge of the lessons of the past that provide a pathway to the future. He stays in each sign for two and a half years but works in cycles of seven. His collective message can be measured as he moves from sign to sign, initiating new lessons for all of us at once by concentrating his energy in one place. In your personal chart, however, he gives you two and a half years to figure out the essence of each of his twelve lessons. Saturn, as your cosmic schoolmaster, offers you constant immersion in his dense life texts. As he moves through the sky, he comes to visit all the classrooms of your existence. Later in this section, we will show you how to figure out where he is right now and where he'll be for the rest of your life. The Saturn Return is the perfect opportunity to meet him. At this moment he's in a very serious mood, ruler in hand, ready to inflict corporeal punishment if you don't sit up straight and answer the question.

Joseph Campbell famously urged us: "Follow your bliss." He taught that we usually suffer to the degree we have fallen off "the beam" in our lives and have given our authority away to an external system. A Saturn lesson can come disguised in a Darth Vader costume, commanding us to accept the security of a worldly, mechanical system luring us with false power. Ultimately, Saturn is our life. He assesses us and asks us to really look at ourselves. He asks us, "Are you on the beam?" He wants us to use the force within and to become the heroes of our journey.

Saturn, the Roman god, got his assignation because he was associated with the Greek god Kronos, father of Zeus. Kronos so feared losing his authority to his son that he ate his children. This story shows the ugliest side of Saturn. Here, he is at his worst—fierce, unconscious, and unbridled. In our time, Saturn continues to be feared and revered, but we want you to look at his good side, his potential to heal us. He appears as a demon only when we refuse to acknowledge him, to look him square in the eye and meet his fearsome stare. He embodies the teaching, "Whatever doesn't kill you makes you stronger."

If we look at the mythological cast of characters, including Saturn, as members of our own psychological theater troupe, as Carl Jung did, we can see that a symbolic will to power (a desire to exercise authority over others) can have drastic consequences. This can happen in dreams or in our waking lives. In the story of Saturn eating his children, he didn't want to give up the gig as master of his domain. Saturn will seem to devour us if we lord our power over others. This is not a pretty picture. (One of the most terrifying images of Saturn can be found on the walls of the Museo del Prado, in Madrid. Goya's famous painting *Saturn Devorando a un Hijo* hangs there. It shows a wild-eyed monster-man devouring a human body, head first. Blood and darkness are the primary themes.) When Saturn shows up as a painful lesson, it is often about clinging to used-up, restrictive, rigid old structures that no longer function. His influence can feel like rules for rules' sake, but truly there is always a lesson underneath. And it's a powerful lesson, one that is usually fated and part of the karmic package we've all signed up for. Liz Greene, in her book *Saturn: A New Look at an Old Devil*, said it best: "Whether we use psychological or esoteric terminology, the basic fact remains the same: human beings do not earn free will except through self-discovery, and they do not attempt self-discovery until things become so painful that they have no other choice." This is the domain of Saturn.

Saturn and Karma

Carl Jung said: "That which we do not bring to consciousness appears in our lives as fate." Saturn is probably the least-liked fate, showing up to greet you as a policeman, a tyrannical boss, or even a cruel, chastising lover or friend. A great Saturnian teacher of India, Vimalanda, has said:

> Saturn is the force of fate, the force that makes you experience your karmas whether you want to or not. In fact, he is the planet in charge of experience. Until you have completely conquered

your innate nature, Saturn can still affect you. Saturn will search out the weaknesses in your personality and expose them to full view, making you experience your limitations by making your ego self-identify with those limitations.

In other words, Saturn throws us back on ourselves again and again until we learn to own and define our limits, own our yeses and our noes (he's not thrilled with fence-sitting, where other people decide our fate for us). He forces us to face our weaknesses (instead of making excuses, blaming others, or hoping someone else will pay for the consequences of our actions) and conquer them through willpower, discipline, and constructive action and then make our own rules. Ultimately, Saturn asks us to own our own authority while remaining humble. He teaches us humility and endurance.

Saturn has been called the essence of misery. But all of the suffering he brings exists to strengthen and humble us. In the movie *Frida*, Frida Kahlo, artist and Saturn-survivor, said: "At the end of the day we can endure a lot more than we thought we could." This is the heart of Saturn's teaching.

Faith is vital when reeling from the Saturn Return. Doubt is one of Saturn's greatest weapons. He will make us doubt ourselves on every level until we are rock solid and know how to define our life. If we base our self-worth on the outer world's symbols without sifting it through our inner Saturn-sieve, we will be waylaid until we get it right. Saturn drops leaden bombs around us until we get back to our inner dictums and rhythms.

How to Use This Book— Understanding the Twelve Lessons of Saturn

All that we've discussed tells us why Saturn transits often feel so uncomfortable. Transits occur as planets travel the solar system and form angles to the planets of your natal chart. The Saturn Return is simply a transit of Saturn to the natal chart, albeit one of the most infamous and important. As Saturn moves through the zodiac, he hangs out in each constellation for about two and a half years and thus touches your chart someplace, effectively making you feel like complete crap in that area of your life. Imagine him standing there in the shadow of your living room barking orders. Wherever he has most recently come to visit your chart is where you'll hear his saber rattling. To get an idea of how this works, take a look at Figure 1. Think of it as a pie—an often delicious, warm, sweet pie filled with some unexpected ingredients, possibly a nail or a grenade, an asshole boyfriend or two, and something delicious on top, but only if you work for your dessert. That's your life, baby, in that circle. Your own personal chart looks quite like Figure 1. All of the slices represent different areas of your life, and that's how we've organized this book. The twelve lessons of Saturn correspond to the twelve signs of the zodiac and to the twelve sectors of your existence. The first slice, "Persona," is about initiation, aggression, and the quest for identity. It concerns the way we assert ourselves and the way we handle aggression and impulsive tendencies. The second, "Attachment," is about the desires and habits that block our creative voice—food and shopping addiction and whatever keeps us stuck in a rut. It is also about owning our values. The third, "The Mind," is about our fear of leaving the whimsy of childhood where we can have our cake and eat it too. It's about our fear of communicating our truth, facing our inner contradictions, and becoming powerful messengers in our lives. The fourth, "Home," is about our roots, our childhood, and our karma with our mother, her side of the family, and the feminine side of our psyche. The fifth, "Creativity," is about embracing our multidimensional creative potential, fear of risk taking, and fear of pleasure. The sixth, "Purification," is about the struggle of simplicity, organization, our various neuroses, and work as service. It is also about the minutiae of the daily grind. The seventh, "The Other," concerns how we deal with our one-to-one relationships—lovers, friends, and the like. The eighth, "Transformation," is about sex, debt (karmic and otherwise), and resisting the changes necessary to undergo complete metamorphosis. The ninth, "Higher Mind," is about how we get out of the confines of our head and into the wisdom of our mind. It's about the gypsy spirit and stretching just beyond the horizon to see what is on the other side. The tenth, "The World," is about getting to the top—of our career, our worldly standing, our status. The eleventh, "Community," is about preserving individuality while joining with a collective force, breaking with convention, and experimenting until the future is brought into the present. It asks, "How do you dare?" It's also about friends, the social world, and group situations. The twelfth and final slice/chapter is "The Source." It's about the deepest depths of the psyche, our dreams, and transcendence.

Saturn comes to visit you in each of these sectors at some point in your life, as his stay in each sign lasts about two and a half years. So you'll face him head-on in every area of your life, even if you don't want to. If you don't really, really get the essence of his lesson after seven years, he'll break out the reality whip, forcing you to shit or get off the pot. (This is where the famous seven-year itch comes from.) He operates in this divine number (also connected to the days in our week, the number of chakras or spiritual energy centers along the spine, and the number of visible planets in the sky).

The Saturn Return, because it represents his return to the place he lived when you made your first appearance on earth, begins at approximately age twenty-nine and a half (this is the length of time it takes him to traverse the whole zodiac).

At the Saturn Return the visit he makes is of grave importance. It's your chance to learn the karmic lessons that Saturn had in mind for you when you decided to incarnate. Just as you are approaching your thirtieth year, he will start to hammer you until you can speak his language with absolute fluency.

We're not going to make you crazy with astrological jargon, because this book is mostly about the areas of your life that Saturn touches as he travels, making loud noises and stomping like a dictator. The hot zone of the Saturn Return occurs approximately from ages twenty-eight to thirty. In reality, one begins to feel the impact of Saturn's imminent hit several years before, as he offers warnings of his arrival. They are generally not heeded until the Saturn Return hits for real. That's why we had to write this book—to get you girls to listen up.

The Cycles of Saturn

As mentioned earlier, Saturn works in seven-year cycles. Look back at your life and carefully consider your seventh year, your fourteenth, and your twenty-first. Each of these have been pivotal moments in Saturn's trip through your orbit. Think about the events of those years. The crisis you approach as you are about to hit your Saturn Return can be traced back to the events that transpired at each of those fundamental ages. However you handled the crises that cropped up through childhood and adolescence has much bearing on the issues that will arise as you approach your Saturn Return.

You can use this book in several ways. We recommend that you read all the way through, absorbing all of the twelve lessons of Saturn. Each lesson has had, or will have, an impact on your life at some point, because Saturn will stop there and spend a few years hammering away at you until you get his point. We will refer to your Saturn placement, or lesson, throughout the book. This is where Saturn started his trip in your life, where he has set up your karmic rule book. This is the central theme, the most important element for you to understand. But because he transits your entire chart, it is extremely helpful to know where he is headed next. At your Saturn Return, he is at the pivotal point where your birth lesson comes to bear again. You will want to pay special attention to the chapters that correspond directly to your specific return and your natal placement of Saturn. (These are likely to resonate the most.) This is as simple as finding out where Saturn was when you were born. You can get a chart at our website (saturn return.net), or take a look at Figure 2. This will show you what sign Saturn lived in when you were born. We recommend that you log on to the site, however, because it will give you even more information. If you know your exact birth time, you can also find out the house Saturn sat in at the moment of your birth, giving you two chapters to underline with a red marker and gasp with recognition as you read, making a spectacle of yourself as you sit in your local cafe. (We recommend this type of behavior. It frees the soul. Without humor, we lose the warmth embedded beneath Saturn's cold, harsh exterior and experience only the fascist side of his energy. He wants us to take our-

---

FIGURE 2   Where is Saturn? Use this chart to determine where Saturn was when you were born . . . and where he's going.

Saturn was in Aries from
March 4, 1967, to April 29, 1969
April 8, 1996, to June 9, 1998
October 26, 1998, to February 28, 1999

Saturn was in Taurus from
April 30, 1969, to June 18, 1971
January 11, 1972, to February 21, 1972
June 10, 1998, to October 25, 1998
March 1, 1999, to August 9, 2000
October 17, 2000, to April 20, 2001

Saturn was in Gemini from
June 19, 1971, to January 10, 1972
February 22, 1972, to August 1, 1973
January 8, 1974, to April 18, 1974
August 10, 2000, to October 16, 2000
April 21, 2001, to June 4, 2003

Saturn was in Cancer from
August 2, 1973, to January 7, 1974
April 19, 1974, to September 17, 1975
January 15, 1976, to June 5, 1976
Saturn will be in Cancer from June 5,
    2003, to July 16, 2005

Saturn was in Leo from
September 18, 1975, to January 14, 1976
June 6, 1976, to November 17, 1977
January 6, 1978, to July 26, 1978
Saturn will be in Leo from July 17, 2005,
    to September 2, 2007

Saturn was in Virgo from
November 18, 1977, to January 5, 1978
July 27, 1978, to September 21, 1980
Saturn will be in Virgo from September 3,
    2007, to October 29, 2009, and from
    April 8, 2010, to July 21, 2010

Saturn was in Libra from
September 22, 1980, to November 29,
    1982
May 7, 1983, to August 24, 1983
Saturn will be in Libra from October 30,
    2009, to April 7, 2010, and July 22,
    2010, to October 5, 2012

Saturn was in Scorpio from
November 30, 1982, to May 6, 1983
August 25, 1983, to November 17, 1985

Saturn was in Sagittarius from
November 18, 1985, to February 13,
    1988
June 11, 1988, to November 12, 1988

Saturn was in Capricorn from
January 6, 1959, to January 3, 1962
February 14, 1988, to June 10, 1988
November 13, 1988, to February 6, 1991

Saturn was in Aquarius from
January 4, 1962, to March 24, 1964
September 18, to December 16, 1964
February 7, 1991, to May 20, 1993
July 1, 1993, to January 28, 1994

Saturn was in Pisces from
March 25, 1964, to September 17, 1964
December 17, 1964, to March 3, 1967
May 21, 1993, to June 30, 1993
January 29, 1994, to April 7, 1996

selves seriously so that we earn the right to laugh at and with ourselves.)

Breaking It Down

Each chapter begins with a series of questions that are likely to resonate with you if you were born into a particular lesson of Saturn (by either sign or house) *or* if Saturn is coming around to visit you in a new area of your chart. That's why this book is useful even if you're not going through your Saturn Return right now. If you're a few years past it, or if it's still a few years away, Saturn still matters in your life. (This is why you should really read the whole book. Saturn doesn't want you to be lazy.) The first half of each chapter describes the general characteristics of the Saturn lesson across the lifetime. So, if you were born with Saturn in Aries or Saturn in the first house, you are likely to relate to the issues and examples detailed in the first half of the chapter. This is the broad analysis part of the chapter. You might relate to some sections as if we snuck into your brain and stole your story. On the other hand, some sections could feel a little foreign. That's the big Saturn caveat. (It's the caveat for all astrology, actually.) Don't get mad at us if it's not all absolutely, unequivocally true. Some stuff will be foreign, and some will be freakishly familiar.

Next, we address father issues relating to each Saturn lesson. Because Saturn is symbolic of the Father (in the universal sense), his placement in your chart tends to deeply influence your relationship with the man you call "Dad." In each chapter, we outline some of the problems and more pleasant potentials portended by Saturn's placement with respect to your father and his impact on your life. Remember, we are talking about *your* Saturn placement, not your dad's. (You can look up his Saturn placement later if you want and offer him some helpful insight.) For example, if you were born with Saturn in Aries, your relationship with your father might be fraught with all of the good and bad qualities of Aries—aggression, power struggles, and insecurity.

The third segment of each chapter concerns the Saturn Return itself and what you might experience while you're under its weighty influence. The last part of each chapter is dedicated to real-world Saturn stories, actual narratives about our clients. They illustrate experiences common to each Saturn placement, first in childhood and adolescence, and then through to the Saturn Return and beyond.

Surviving the Saturn Return

Whether you are about to endure the transition, are in the last few moments of your twenties, or have safely crossed the threshold and found (whew!) that a few crow's-feet have not carried you to your death, you are already surviving your Saturn Return. If you are honest with yourself, you can admit that this is tough stuff. If you like to play pretend, your repression is likely to creep up and bite you when you least expect it.

Saturn is a drill sergeant of sorts, the one who forces you to get in line. If you don't follow his orders, you pay the consequences by being forced to clean the dirty toilet bowl of your life with an old toothbrush. The trick is, you must learn to love him even as he spits in your face and calls you names. Reading this book will assist you with mastering this lesson.

This book is a first, for women and astrologers both. Men experience Saturn Returns as well, but we chose to focus on women's experiences. We believe that the planets affect us in entirely different ways. There is no astrology book to date exploring the phenomenon of the Saturn Return, and we thought it was about time. It is, indeed, a huge astrological event for all of us, and understanding it is half the battle of surviving it. We hope this book will honor the greatness of Saturn yet reveal what an important, albeit fierce, ally he can be.

We wrote this book because at twenty-seven both of us began to feel the creeping threat of imminent nervous breakdowns. At first we ascribed these feelings to the sociocultural implications of turning thirty. But being astrologers, we had an advantage—we knew that what we were feeling wasn't simply fear of aging. We started to ask around and began to witness a pattern among our friends. We checked their Saturn placements, and in every case, it made sense. Their unique circumstances matched the place where Saturn sat in their chart. We have consulted hundreds of post–Saturn Return women while researching this book. In every case, there has been a crisis that turned into a chrysalis, as Jungian psychoanalyst Marion Woodman says. We promise that whatever you are going through, on the other side of this transition is a transformation.

Aries

Aries needs action. Aries needs to be first. Aries needs fierce passion. Aries needs self-knowledge. Aries needs to charge ahead of the rest. Aries needs healthy competition. Aries needs power. Aries needs to dance with her spear, to fight to the death, to burst forward like a flame. Aries needs to be the inferno. Aries needs it yesterday. Aries needs to butt heads. Aries needs to win the game. Aries needs to set it all on fire. Aries needs to initiate. Aries needs the lightning rod. Aries needs never to wait.

Persona

ARIES

Keywords/Issues:	initiative, activity, enterprise, aggression, drive, impulse, adventure
Ruler:	Mars
Symbol:	The Ram
Element:	Fire
Modality:	Cardinal
Opposite:	Libra
Archetype:	The Emperor
Key Phrase:	I Am
	Aries rules the head
	Aries is associated with the first house

For one who knows Reality, the whole world is her wealth. She cannot see anything different from her own Self.

—MATA AMRITANANDAMAYI

Aries is the very first sign of the zodiac, and you better watch yourself when she comes around with her torch. This is where you find the screaming infant, straight out of the birth canal, ready to march forward into life. She is red, burning with radiance, fierce, and passionate. If you were born into the Saturn in Aries lesson, you probably feel this intense, ecstatic burn deep inside, this need for action. But Saturn here has a way of making you feel as if you can't stand the heat. Rather than propelling you forward into the mighty fires of initiation, when Saturn lands in Aries, you could, instead, end up feeling a bit burnt out. We don't suggest you get out of the kitchen, firewoman. Instead we invite you to put your lovely hand over the flame and risk getting a little bit scorched. It won't hurt nearly as much as you think.

If you were born with Saturn in Aries or Saturn in the first house, or if Saturn is coming around the mountain to smite you in this area of your chart, you might ask yourself the following questions:

- How are you at first impressions?
- Do you spend enough time getting to know who you are?
- Are you afraid of being called selfish?
- Do you suffer from low self-esteem or harbor repressed rage?
- Do you have major issues with the way you look?
- What would you do if there were no more mirrors?
- Do you find it difficult to assert yourself?
- Are you ever your own worst enemy?
- Do you wear a mask to protect yourself from the outside world?

The Saturn in Aries lesson is about your mask, your persona, and the image you project to the world. When you are consumed with self-image, it's hard to separate the outside and the inside. When your ego is assaulted, your heart is, too. You could tend to turn your frustration into a self-consuming conflagration. Please don't become a martyr for Saturn and immolate yourself on his altar. We will guide you out of the burning building of your Saturn placement. Follow us and remain calm.

Hit Me With Your Best Shot

One of the fundamental aspects of this lesson, if you were presented with it at birth, is that you are likely to be on the defensive much of the time. You may feel that an assault is always imminent (Aries is the warrior) and keep your spear ready at all moments. Conversations can be battlegrounds, because you often expect people to throw daggers your way. Instead, you're apt to shoot first, come what may. This might get you into a fair amount of trouble some of the time. With this lesson, though, you are seeking true and natural self-confidence, not false ego posturing. A bit of pugilism is probably part of your package. You've got a little Muhammad Ali in your soul, girl.

She's So Shy

If you were born into this lesson, another possibility is that you're terribly shy and have created a serious shield so that those you meet will never know that you're shaking inside, lest they discover the true you. This is just one of the dangers of avoiding your Saturn lesson—if you don't work on distinguishing the inside from the outside, being honest about it, and loving both halves of yourself, you could become so overidentified with the persona that you'll forget who you really are. Saturn in Aries sometimes makes you feel that cultivating the persona is the sole focus, and a lot of inner growth can be lost to the art of external excellence. This shyness can be severe and might start early in life. People could interpret your shyness as arrogance. And you may have even built some actual arrogant armor around you so that others won't be able to peer inside. Do others experience you as a bit of a snob? Even if you're the kindest girl on the block, open to all types, with not an obnoxious bone in your body, you could be perceived as a world-class snot. When people drink in a first impression of you, it could very well be that you think you're the greatest. You may project that kind of vibe because you're just a little scared and shy, and you really, really want everybody to like you. (And to like you the best.)

First Come, First Served

If you were born into this lesson, you are learning to be first, and to feel good about it. Secretly, you may yearn to push ahead and cut to the front of the line, but you might find yourself deferring, deferring, deferring to the needs of others rather than taking up space at the table yourself. This can cause all sorts of physical problems, headaches in particular. Try not to destroy yourself slowly by repressing your natural anger and aggression. The healthiest solution for you as the Saturn in Aries woman is to let yourself feel the anger, but that's easier said than done. The polarity that plagues you concerns your thwarted need to lead the parade. It bucks up against Saturn's constant naysaying. Your deepest instinct may be telling you to rush into the fray, but Saturn is apt to layer some heavy-duty, death-defying guilt over that urge to charge over all obstacles. The cure is to just do it. This should be *your* slogan, not Nike's.

Why Me?

If you were marked by this lesson at birth, you could feel as if the world is always against you, but if we sliced open your psyche with our magical psychological paring knife, you'd probably see clearly that you have waged war against yourself. There might be a sense that you are surrounded by selfishness at every turn. Why, you may wonder, am I attracting such self-absorbed people into my life? In reality, you may be the true control freak. What sucks is that the folks that we attract into our lives have a lot to tell us about who we are, what we need, and what we are likely to become—not fun to acknowledge when your buddy is being an asshole. But next time your friend pisses you off because she's too busy thinking about herself, take a look in your nearest mirror. What is she teaching you? For you, especially, it's important to measure the natures of those that you are close to, because they are careful barometers for your own needs. (The Saturn in Libra lesson has a similar effect.)

Firefighter

Power, or lack thereof, could be a fundamental theme in your life. Because you are learning to embrace your inner warrior, you might find yourself entangled in constant power struggles, learning to assert your will in all of your relationships, major and minor. Your domestic struggles can reflect this inner need as surely as a battle waged with the checkout person at the supermarket. Saturn is constantly testing you, trying to get you to see that you are truly, beautifully powerful, in healthy ways. He'll also show you where you fight too hard and exhaust yourself needlessly, all in the pursuit of safety. You may feel as if you were born to be a battering ram, and this stance can inform every one of your interactions. You may even have some violent tendencies. You don't want to turn into Hannibal with a manicure. Be careful. Mostly you contain yourself, but there are things that can send you over the edge, particularly if you've been holding it in too long.

Question Authority

This may be your favorite bumper sticker. And it's a healthy attitude, if not taken too far. But you may have at least once broken rank and yelled right into your boss's face, just to make a point. You might be terrified of being controlled. And this can set you up for failure, or at least what you perceive as failure. You may carry quite a chip on your shoulder, and this chip can grow in size so much through your lifetime that by the time you reach your SR, it could very well topple you over. You might feel as if you always fail. If this is the case, perhaps you set yourself up for failure, because you can't figure out how to believe in yourself. The moment that you get that you are talented, beautiful, smart, and capable is the moment that the world will agree with you. The praise and promotion you seek will fall into place like a set of shiny dominoes. Pretending to be OK on the outside while throwing a raging temper tantrum on the inside, all because you don't think you're good enough, will keep your dreams at a distance.

I Feel Pretty

Are you willing to endure pain to be beautiful? The Saturn in Aries lesson is all about self-image. It teaches you how to really like yourself. But before you get there, you may go through a crucible of self-hate that is hotter than hell itself. Saturn here is notorious for making your body into a punching bag for all of society's very favorite "beauty" treatments. Do you use Botox? Do you undergo liposuction? Do you suffer through dermabrasion? For some women born into the Saturn in Aries lesson, no procedure is too painful to preserve external beauty. You might feel as if you are nothing without your face on.

The other possibility, and one that makes us sad, is that you could be the sort to starve yourself or become bulimic to attain perfection. All body image issues are common here—just about anywhere on the continuum. Body dysmorphic disorder, a disease in which you see physical flaws in an exaggerated and somewhat pathological way, is a possibility. This could be your cross to bear, and at the SR, a crisis around this issue might just make you wake up and stop being mean to yourself.

Famous People with Saturn in Aries/First House

Bette Davis

Jennifer Aniston

Julia Roberts

Helen Keller

Cher

Gwen Stefani

I Think I Can, I Think I Can . . .

Astrologer Bil Tierney calls your syndrome "stage fright of the soul." It can cause you to suffer from deep depressions from time to time. Some Saturn in Aries women have chronic bouts of depression. When you are constantly fighting with your inner nature, your desire to take off like a flame and go forth, the result can be sadness and longing. The energy of Saturn and the energy of Aries are really at odds with one another. Saturn tells you to sit down and calculate, to measure, to take it slow. Aries tells you to charge off into the wilderness, screaming all of your desires to the wind, or to anyone within listening distance. It's not an easy fit, and it can make you feel as if you're being taken on a nausea-inducing ride.

You might carry around an anxiety about spontaneity that causes you to plan everything out. You could be afraid to move and change, even to make changes that you know will be good for you. You're likely to constantly question yourself and have trouble accepting that you'll be able to follow through and complete any project. Those born with their sun in Aries are notorious for starting eight projects at once, on a whim, just because. Then the projects are abandoned just as quickly in favor of the next new thing. But with Saturn here, you may find that you're afraid to even get started. You may not be able to wrangle yourself out of the gate, let alone start running. This can cause a self-resentment of sorts to build in you. It would do you well to repeat, "I think I can, I think I can . . ." like the little engine that could. This is the perfect mantra to help guide the Saturn in Aries lady through the dark nights of her soul.

Close to Me

Another problem wrought by this lesson is the inability to get really close to anyone who wants to know you well. How could you possibly do so, when you feel like the ugly duckling inside? You are number one when it comes to building walls to your inner world. You might do whatever it takes to blot out any indication that you feel inadequate, trying to convince paramours and friends that all's cool with school. Really, you are likely convinced that the school needs a new principal and all the teachers should be fired *tout de suite*, but you're not apt to make this announcement over the loudspeakers. Instead, you smile your best disarming smile (while inside you criticize yourself that it's lopsided) and hope that your companions don't notice the bricks spilling out of your supporting walls. It's hard for people to know who you really are inside. When you do allow people to get close, it's usually because you've inoculated yourself against their judgments, or they've somehow proved to you that they are not the sort that would judge at all. A lot of folks might find you a bit standoffish, but this is the classic protective shyness. You are dying for adulation, for someone to tell you that you are really all right, but it's hard for you to let anyone get near enough to you to see what's underneath the facade. You probably have trouble asking for what you want, because deep inside you feel as if you don't deserve it.

Father Issues with Saturn in Aries

Did your daddy have a bad temper? Or did he repress his rage most of the time, until the moment that it erupted like Vesuvius? Was he egotistical? Did he bang the table to demand his dinner? Was he loud and brash and sometimes embarrassing? Did he make you feel as if being pretty was the most important way to please him? When born into the Saturn in Aries lesson, little girls often deal with dads that fit this mold. Fathers are often impulsive, impatient, and too fiery for their own good. Saturn in Aries daughters sometimes carry tremendous stores of repressed anger toward their dads for their various offenses. If he was unavailable, many of your life lessons might be built around your fury at him. Or maybe you want to get back at him for all the times he yelled at you. Often Saturn in Aries dads are the type that consciously or unconsciously make you feel very insecure. This type of dad might make you feel less than beautiful or suggest subtly that your course through life would be greatly enhanced by working on your good looks. He may have evaluated you on your physical qualities, causing this issue to rear its head over and over again throughout your life.

On the other hand, maybe he spurred you on to success. Perhaps he was behind you all the time, lighting that fire under your ass. He may have urged you, perhaps too hard, to be number one. Was he your cheerleader? He may have donned those dad pom-poms one too many times for your liking. Maybe he meant well, but you may have felt undue pressure. Did he push you to be a self-starter? Was he disappointed when you weren't first? Did he chant "You're number one. You're number one."? If you came in second, did he give you guilt? He may have treated you a little bit like a burgeoning boy. Did spending time with him ever feel as if you were training for a marathon? If he pushed you, you may have resented him for it. And anger management may have been a big issue for your dad, and for your relationship with him. Whether he kept it in or let it out, his anger issues are likely to have created a legacy for you. Letting out your fury toward your dad, if you're harboring any, could be just what you need. Beat a pillow and give him your best hyena howl. There, there. You might find, though, that confronting him directly, if possible, whether through a letter or another means, is the only thing that really releases you from his hold.

Facing the Saturn Return with Saturn in Aries

Once you hit your SR, your crisis could feel quite volcanic. Years of wearing masks, hiding your feelings, and repressing your anger can catch up with you. Often, at the SR, Saturn in Aries women experience an issue with an authority figure that grows out of hand. You might decide that you can't take it anymore and give it to your boss. You might start to feel ready to confront someone or something that you feel has been holding you back from your true glory. You might break down and start to long for the deeply buried beautiful treasures that you blocked from view. But this usually happens through some sort of seemingly external source that first seems to wreck you. Criticism of your performance at work, a thinly veiled critique of your looks, or some other experience can feel like an attack from a monster whose only interest is to bring you down. This monster is called Big Daddy Saturn, and what you must know is that he doesn't really want to bring you down. He wants you to see the silver hidden under years of tarnish. This is your opportunity to break out the polish and get to looking for your true reflection in that self-hating knife of yours.

This could diminish your vitality, and depression could result. Another possibility is that your confidence will be rocked by a loss of prestige. Sometimes Saturn in Aries women lose jobs at the SR, those that were all glitter and no substance. You may have seemed to have it all together at the top of the heap, but Saturn could storm in at the SR and show you the superficial cracks in your job armor. You may realize that that fancy office is not all you thought it was at first. Instead, you may start to reevaluate and find that appearing attractive and polished is less important than you thought.

Power struggles are also apt to play out at the SR. If you are giving all your power away in a relationship, or playing the role of sadist yourself, you may find that the SR won't allow your soul to sustain the imbalances. Someone who has lived idly under your thumb is unlikely to allow this to continue. If you've been letting someone control you for way too long, you may not be able to stand it anymore when your SR comes along. You can take back your rightful power now and recognize if you've been hoarding it.

Start Me Up

One of the gifts of the SR for those born into the Saturn in Aries lesson is that you can really get to know yourself now. It's likely that Saturn has blocked your instinctual energies for most of your life, and when he comes back around at the SR, he is giving you another chance to focus on them. You might feel terrified of doing so, more so than ever before, but an event is likely to occur to make sure that you look at what's going on inside. Scream therapy might be a great tool for you right now, or kickboxing, or any activity that allows you to get in touch with your inner warrior. You need to take action at this time, and not in unnatural ways. Channeling your energies into healthy forms, rather than giving in to the urge to punch out your boyfriend, will serve you well. A lot of Saturn in Aries women develop severe migraines, have hot flashes, and get skin rashes and breakouts at the SR. These are signs that you're not dealing with the psychological issues at hand but rather letting them attack you from the inside, without consciousness. Physical activity can help you figure what's going on inside of you as well. If you are in talk therapy, consider adding movement to the mix. Action melts blocks caused by Saturn's placement in Aries, so even when you feel afraid to make a move, literal or metaphoric, you can heal yourself by facing the fear and plunging in, headfirst.

Real-World Saturn Return in Aries Stories

Jennifer: The Ugly Duckling Syndrome

One experience Jennifer recalls from childhood was the moment in second grade when Tommy, the school bully, teased her about her hair. She had mismatched barrettes in, an oversight of her mother's, and hadn't thought about it until Tommy called her attention to her lack of color coordination. Rather than defending herself, she blushed and looked down, and felt as if everyone on the playground was looking at her. She felt ugly and out of place, the first of many similar moments. Tommy tortured her for the entire year, until he moved to another school district. But that year was enough to tattoo this disturbing memory in her consciousness. He attacked her hair, her nose, her teeth, her sneakers, just about anything he could identify. Obviously it was just because he liked her, but Jennifer felt ostracized and became hyperaware of the way she put herself together in the mornings. She began to ask her mother to take her to certain stores, and she refused to wear the items that Tommy had teased her about.

In junior high she endured the standard series of awkward physical humiliations, plus clear braces that turned yellow and an early gangliness. She started walking hunched over by seventh grade, as she sprouted many inches above her peers. She wanted to be totally invisible in front of boys, and she felt as if all they noticed were her endless faults. She would go home and gaze in the mirror for hours and hours, trying desperately to figure out how to hide her perceived flaws. By ninth grade she was bingeing and purging, plagued by the belief that if she could only perfect her body all would be right with the world. But it wasn't just her weight that obsessed her. As the years wore on, she trained her angry gaze on her nose—too long, her feet—too big, her skin—too freckled, and on and on. She spent all of her baby-sitting money on cosmetics, diet pills, and fashion magazines. Although she was smart, rather than concentrate on studies, she focused on becoming beautiful. Her father had always praised her for being "Daddy's pretty girl" when she was a young child, and it was the only kind of attention that he gave her. Otherwise, he seemed angry all the time, but for the moments when he praised her beauty. This sort of attention was all she knew and all she could chase after.

By the time she reached college, she felt as if she caught at least part of a brass ring. Finally, her height was a bonus. Guys turned to look at her. She was a makeup genius and had learned the art of the perfect outfit. She was always put together. She got a lot of attention. Still, inside, she felt defiantly ugly.

Right out of college she landed a job in public relations. Everything was fabulous. She was promoted every year, went to parties, wore designer clothes, and was the envy of many. But still, she felt as if no one knew her. She had many friends, but with all of them she felt that she had to be "on" all the time. Right before the onset of her SR, at twenty-seven, Jennifer was starting to feel less than thrilled about her work conditions. The owner of the firm was getting on her nerves, and she felt micromanaged. She began to feel that her line of work was petty and vapid. It didn't feel so fabulous anymore. She didn't want to dress up in Prada and perform all day long. But she needed the job and resolved to stay there until something better came along. She had no idea what she would pursue if she left the industry, anyway. She went on this way, vaguely unhappy, until her SR became active when she was almost twenty-nine. One day she arrived at work to find that her boss's assistant was waiting for her with an urgent message. She was ushered into his office and sat down. He was glaring. He yelled at her and fired her on the spot for a mistake she'd made the week before with a big client. She had to leave that day, with all her things in a box. She was so devastated that she hid in her house for four months. She didn't want to get dressed, to network, to go to parties. She fell into a deep depression and had no idea what she would do next with her life. She felt as if everything she knew was stripped from her—her whole identity torn away. More than anything, she felt desperately ugly, this time on the surface, too. She was so depressed that things that usually fed her—manicures, facials, and shopping sprees—were totally unappealing. She loafed around in sweat clothes and felt sorry for herself.

At the behest of a friend, Jennifer finally decided to take a look at her life, after four months on the couch. She tried a new couch—that is, the therapist's couch. She started somatic therapy and in the process discovered deep wells of repressed resentment. She spent a lot of time punching the air and screaming, and she released many buried demons. Soon she realized that she'd been hiding her whole life. Her persona had consumed her, and she didn't know who she was anymore. It took her SR to get her to chip away at the layers and layers of protective armor she'd built through the years. By the time she turned thirty and her SR was over, she knew that PR was not the right field for her, not even close. She worked toward rebuilding her self-esteem and learned that she had much to give even if she wasn't flawless on the outside. Now, at thirty-three, Jennifer has a new career as a chef and has left her old life behind completely. Cooking didn't seem glamorous enough to her before the SR, and she wouldn't acknowledge that this was actually her hidden dream. She rarely obsesses about her appearance these days, and she feels fulfilled by her new work.

Arlene: Power Struggles

Arlene was born into difficult circumstances. Her father died when she was an infant, and her mother struggled to raise her on her own until Arlene was six. At that point her mother met Steve, a new boyfriend, and he moved in right away. Steve was Arlene's instant nemesis. He had violent tendencies, and she was afraid to be alone with him. Still, having had no father figure for the first six years of her life, she longed for his approval. He never told her she was smart or capable, and he said nice things only about her looks. She was a very cute little girl and got a lot of attention for her golden curly hair and big blue eyes.

Arlene found herself alone with Steve way too often, and as she got older, she grew more afraid of him. He

Survival Skills for Saturn in Aries

Take risks.

Play with matches. (Just kidding!)

Study martial arts.

Initiate.

Try scream therapy.

Assert yourself.

Cover all the mirrors in your home for one day.

Try boxing.

Approach someone who makes you feel shy.

Know how beautiful you are.

seemed to get angrier as she aged. She recoiled sometimes when he came near her, afraid of the back of his hand and his angry words. She watched him sometimes as he slammed his fist into doors, broke things, and expressed his poorly managed anger in myriad physical ways. Arlene repressed her own feelings of anger and fear, and she kowtowed to Steve constantly. She developed a severe problem with shyness.

Her teen years were spent in pursuit of escape, and she made hers early, at seventeen. Knowing that she had to get out or die, she got into an early acceptance program and went clear across the country to attend college. There she met her boyfriend, Andy, and quickly fell in love with him. She neglected to notice that he had violent tendencies of his own. At first he didn't turn them on her. He yelled at waiters, at other drivers, and sometimes at his dog. It always made her skin crawl, but he said he loved her and she couldn't imagine anyone else keeping her around. She felt blessed to be with Andy, a boy so good looking and charming. She looked in the mirror sometimes and wondered what he was doing with her in the first place.

The first time he hit her he was drunk and instantly sorry. She ran out but couldn't stay away. She came back the next day, he begged for mercy, and she believed him when he said he wouldn't do it again. But it did happen again, two months later. This time it was worse. She had to live with a bruise on her cheek, and she tried desperately to camouflage it with foundation. But it didn't work, and one of her professors took her aside to talk. She wasn't ready to admit that she was addicted to this abusive cycle and claimed to have fallen in the snow.

She stayed with Andy for seven years. He continued to react with rage even in the face of the smallest indiscretion. He turned on her with cruel words, and once every few months, he became violent. The relationship was desperately toxic, and it was killing her. She hadn't the self-esteem to escape, and she continued to make excuses for him. When she was twenty-eight and her SR started to kick in, she realized what her friends and family had been begging her to recognize since the relationship started. It was as if someone flicked the light switch of her unconscious, and she decided to break up with him. It was the most difficult transition she'd ever made in her life. She cried every day for six months. But at the end of it, her natural power showed itself.

She was able to make a series of changes in her life and no longer desired the company of abusive, aggressive, power-hungry men. At twenty-nine, she began to seek an authentic relationship, and by the end of her SR, she met someone who saw the real her. She wasn't wearing a mask anymore, cowering in the corner. She learned to express her anger heartily and her love fiercely, without restraint. She's thirty-two now, and in a stable, healthy relationship.

Saturn in Aries Potentials

These are a few examples of the way the Saturn in Aries lesson unfolds at the SR. Yours may be a bit different. You might experience problems with authority figures, self-esteem, personal appearance (from eating disorders to body dysmorphic disorder), violence (from within and without), repressed anger, shyness, and the like. There are a variety of ways to heal Saturn in Aries issues. Getting in touch with your warrior side is key. If you don't take the time to express yourself physically, you've got to start now! Start swinging from those monkey bars, become a karate master, and get in touch with your Xena the Warrior Princess self. Taking risks you never would have considered before can be your breakthrough. Go bungee jumping. Get on the back of a motorcycle. Better yet, get in the driver's seat and take off. Go up to the hottest person in the bar and say hi. No one can resist you when you exude the confidence that is your birthright.

You might want to cover the mirrors in your home and go on a cosmetic fast for a week. Leave the house without makeup, particularly if you're afraid of doing so. When you find that your self-confidence steals you more glances than a perfect coiffure ever could, you'll be in business. There's nothing wrong with dressing up pretty, but if you usually rely on your beauty to get places, at the SR, you should risk life without the cosmetics counter. Just as an experiment.

You are fierce. Look in the mirror, recognize your beauty, and tell yourself this. Right now. That's it. Straight to the mirror. Soon this will be your mantra, not mere idle chatter. It's time for truth.

Taurus

Taurus needs routine, the ground, and the stable relationship. Taurus needs a good partner to eat with and sleep with. Taurus needs comfort food. Taurus needs comfort, period, until she learns the glory of discipline. Taurus needs security before she learns self-possession. Taurus needs money before she remembers her inner resources. Taurus needs guarantees before she finds surrender. Taurus needs the predictable until she gets sick of the ruts. Taurus needs the loyal-dog mate until she needs her space. Taurus needs green grass and beautiful gardens to sniff. Taurus needs to own her values and to speak her truth. Taurus needs to sing. Taurus needs a sexy voice. Taurus needs to talk about her meals and her favorite flowers. Taurus needs possession until she feels the burden of baggage.

Attachment

TAURUS

Keywords/Issues:	slow, building, conservative, practical, sensuous, stubborn, self-indulgent, materialistic, patient, lover of beauty, loyal, determined, owning, possessive, calm, affectionate
Ruler:	Venus
Symbol:	The Bull
Element:	Earth
Modality:	Fixed
Opposite:	Scorpio
Archetype:	The High Priest or Hierophant
Key Phrase:	I Have

Taurus rules the ears, mouth, lower jaw, chin, vocal chords, neck, throat, thyroid gland, and base of the skull

Taurus is associated with the second house

Without forsaking the taste of the tongue, one cannot enjoy the taste of the heart.

—MATA AMRITANANDAMAYI

If Saturn was making his way through the sign of the bull when you were born, you probably have a complex relationship to the sensual world and your place within it. If your corporeal instincts are blocked, so is your voice, your creativity, and your time. Taurus is the sign of solidity. Imagine pushing through a pool of deep, rich soil, green shoots just peeking through the crust of the earth. Taurus craves grounding and lush, fertile foundations. But Taurean energies can turn muddy, and especially if you have Saturn here, you can get stuck in the center of them. Saturn can make you to feel a little guilty for indulging in earthly pleasures, so one of the big issues for this lesson is trading off mealtime or sex time for creativity. Saturn can also block or distort natural Taurean tendencies, like having a nice solid bank account . . . or he can teach you how to finally stop holding on to every damned thing past its due. If you were born with Saturn in Taurus or Saturn in the second house, or if Saturn is about to visit you in this sector of your chart, you should consider the following questions:

- What are you afraid to let go of?
- Where are you greedy?
- Do you ever feel stuck in a rut?
- Where are you struggling with money and resources?
- How are you fearful to own your values or time?
- Are you stubborn?
- Are you loyal to a fault?
- How do you feel about your body?
- What is your relationship to food?

How does Saturn, the cosmic disciplinarian, fare in the sign of the firm, practical, possessive bull? As you might understand intuitively, Saturn quite likes adding further grounding and structure to Taurean energy, which is very receptive to discipline. Taurus likes things to be predictable, and with the routine and discipline of Saturn's influence, this is more easily achieved. There might be some conflict of interests between the Taurean need to possess, cling, and indulge when Saturn imposes his deadline to let go, if you are still stuck in that last moment.

On the brighter side, if you are experiencing the Saturn in Taurus lesson, you have great potential to actualize an earthy, grounded approach to life. And you can do the work to get there. Remember, Saturn, as the ruler of time, reminds us that change on the earth plane doesn't happen in an instant. Saturn rules the bones of the body; and it takes seven years for them to restore and renew themselves. Saturn can teach us patience, particularly if we are born into this lesson, and most coherently when we are in the center of our first SR. Taurus is the sign of patience. If we can remind ourselves that it's all just a test, we can find the faith to persevere. Due to the patience and persistence of Taurus, Saturn here often manifests a deeper understanding of the ways in which it pays to stay loyal to long-range plans. In order to do this, Saturn in Taurus teaches us to slow down and exercise some caution in our choices. Do the materials with which we choose to build really define our true values? Yes, those sexy Italian shoes are fabulous, but will they really take you to the next level of your potential? This is the kind of question you may have to ask yourself. Can consumerism really compensate for a deeper need to create? It might make you think again when you contemplate buying the latest item that you fancy behind a glass window, no matter how shiny and tempting it is.

Finding Your Voice

This Saturn lesson tests you on issues around your creative voice and values. Your throat chakra is the energy center for your self-expression and creativity. Examine what shape it's in. Do you suffer from a stiff neck, sore throats, a weak voice, shoulders rising into your ears, or hunchback tendencies? Taurus is very connected to the physical body, thus it is linked with the food we eat. Taurus wants to get us back into our bodies and down to earth. How many of us live in our heads looking down at our bodies less than lovingly? Saturn's energy loves to get us back into our bones, and when he unites with Taurus, he invites us to experience our five senses. Do we take the time to listen to our beloved? To see the sunrise? To taste the food we shovel into our mouths? To smell the flowers? To touch the earth?

The Skinny

One of the most powerful aspects of Saturn's lesson in Taurus is its affect on our relationship to food. As women, we are daily inundated with images of skinny, lifeless models that look as if they haven't eaten in weeks. It goes without saying that women and girls are victims of misogynistic cultural messages about our bodies and how we should treat them. Even if we know intellectually that supermodels and their ilk are not the best arbiters of our self-esteem, even the most enlightened of us can get caught in the trap of "feeling fat" for no reason.

When you're caught in the Saturn in Taurus lesson, you get a double whammy. You may be terrified of food and feeling full. From within and without, you are probably mightily challenged by the desire to feed yourself and the desire to starve yourself, literally and metaphorically. This is one of the classic placements for eating disorders. Bulimia, anorexia, obesity, and everything in between can consume you when you're in this lesson. Any form of eating disorder is common for Saturn in Taurus if the woman does not feel safe and grounded in her own body. When there is a lack of security, the body will become the battleground, and food the weapon.

When you face Saturn, you face the real shape of your body, and the good news is that you can eventually, with some hard work, learn to love it.

Can't Buy Me Love

You probably know that money changes everything. If you don't have it, it plagues you. If you do, you might feel as if it's never enough. The Saturn wound here can create the feeling that you were never provided for, so that becoming your own provider becomes one of the most important quests of your life. Wealth may have been just out of your reach when you were a child. You may have grown up in a wealthy community and had less than the rest of your friends. Or maybe you were the classic "poor little rich girl." Your parents could have given you all the right things to wear, taken you on the best vacations, and brought you to the right restaurants. But this may have stood in for real nourishment. Someone may have tried to buy your love at some point.

You probably want the best, because you understand quality, but you may give up your soul needs to feed your need for finery. Money is probably a prickly issue for you. You want it, lots of it, but you could find that it grows on a thorny bush. You might have a tendency to spend hard-earned cash on unnecessary indulgences instead of on the practical things that Saturn wants you to have. If a beach vacation beckons, with its call of hot sand, the smell of salt, and the taste of fresh seafood, you might empty your bank account for this extravagance instead of upgrading your dinosaur of a computer, something that would improve your productivity and your work life. If it will make you a responsible wage earner, Saturn will applaud. If it will bring pure pleasure at the cost of responsibility, he might throw a wrench in your quest for the sensual and sublime.

Sometimes the Saturn in Taurus lesson causes the opposite defense by declaring that money and material objects are bad, evil, or worthless, and guilt may lead one to deny all forms of material desire and comfort. This is the other extreme: judging all aspects of material comfort either out of fear of the repressed yet overwhelming desire to have it, lack of self-esteem that makes you believe that you don't deserve to have it, or just prior bad experiences resulting from the overemphasis on materialistic values. Somewhere in this twisted manifestation of human complexity lies a simple Saturnian lesson: the true value of anything lies in the self. Money, possessions, ambition, status, food, creature comforts, and so on should not be judged without context. If we project too much of our energy onto material things, we create an inner poverty consciousness.

No Bullshit

Taurus, as the sign of the bull, is classically stereotyped as one of the most stubborn of the signs and is known for its "bull-headed" ways. It is a fixed sign, and when it is linked to Saturn, we can say (because we were both born with it) that this lesson is about the perils of holding on too long. If you refuse to get rid of the stuff that clutters your literal and

Famous People with Saturn in Taurus/Second House

Barbra Streisand

Lucille Ball

Aretha Franklin

Pablo Picasso

metaphoric junk drawer, you will start choking on the accumulated dust. Change is your panacea. You may fear it, but it is the key to your progress.

The Saturn in Taurus lesson can render a stubborn resolve to either master the lessons of time or to stubbornly refuse the change. Change may come to you slowly and with great resistance, but the new structures you build should be solid and permanent. Nothing is to be flimsy or flexible when Saturn meets Taurus. This is but one gift of your placement.

Father Issues with Saturn in Taurus

Did your father collect stuff and more stuff? Or was he the penny-pinching conservative type? Did he down a pint of ice cream, inhale mashed potatoes, or consume other heavy delights from his favorite comfy chair? Was he consistently lecturing you about the value of a dollar or totally out of touch with his own money issues? Perhaps his father was cheap or overly practical or he just inherited some fear of not having enough money. Did he spend recklessly for creature comforts or status goods? Did he overindulge in the world of the senses? Did he refuse change, seemingly stuck in a rut? Maybe you grew up feeling that your dad lacked a solid value system at all. You may have found him totally stubborn and impossible to reason with. This Saturn lesson offers us the "bring me some more beer and potato chips" dad.

On a more positive note, perhaps you felt a real loyalty to your father. He may have been a tried-and-true father figure who was steady and reliable. Or maybe this is what he lacked but what you craved most of all. Your dad may have had a real aesthetic sense and knew how to live in beauty. As long as you define and live by your own values around money, food, and the material world and embrace the art of continual change and letting go, your karmic daddy will have served his purpose.

Facing the Saturn Return with Saturn in Taurus

As Saturn is the "taskmaster" who makes sure we understand our lessons, when he meets with Taurus again at the SR, you must deal with your earth plane issues. This means you must get real about cash, food, and all things connected with the physical body and the five senses. If you really want to learn from the masters, spend some time on a farm with the animals, with no-nonsense folk, and save your pennies. Get yourself a piggy bank, and use it. This is exactly where Saturn will be doing his hard-knocks testing—the most basic of the basic, no-nonsense, meat-and-potatoes issues. Specifically, the tests are going to throw into question issues of a practical nature. Just like the good old conservative father, Saturn in Taurus asks: "Do you really need it?" At first, you may answer, "No, but I want it. I *have* to have it!" As your SR progresses, your answer can shift. Taurus's key phrase is "I have." But what do you *really* have? Truly, you have only that which can't be taken away by natural disaster or other calamities. That basically wipes out all external stuff. Can you live in simplicity and truth, or do you need a fancy wardrobe and big pig helpings to feel safe? Can you rely on your inner resources? If not, you will find Saturn testing you in various earth-spun horror shows, ranging from endless credit card bills to creepy-crawly clutter piles peering out from every corner of your home. Some people with Saturn in Taurus file for bankruptcy or have their homes broken into during their SR.

If you were born into the Saturn in Taurus lesson, the following questions are likely to play on auto reverse in the endless tape deck of your brain during your SR: Do I spend too much? Am I lazy? Am I overly indulgent with food, money, work, or acquiring possessions? Are my possessions and my relationship to the material world in true alignment with my values?

Material resources will challenge you, and your SR can revolve around them. At the SR, anything out of sync will result in restrictions until structural changes are made. Often the inner experience of the host of these issues centers around self-worth. If the feelings of self-worth are too dependent upon money, material status, or possessions (including people) Saturn will remove them in order to see what really sustains you. Interestingly enough, this lesson is often connected with fear of poverty, and sometimes the fear becomes a self-fulfilling prophecy at the SR just to finally move you beyond it. You will likely have the perfect learning opportunity to show you that your personal worth has no basis in the material world. Besides, these objects take up so much space and ruin the feng shui of your psyche. During the SR, many Saturn in Taurus women toss and turn at night in material-istic nightmares that destroy their peace of mind. "Do I really have to get up and go to that horrible job just to pay the bills and get more stuff . . . what is it all for?" Saturn doesn't like it when you hit the sales racks in a frenzy to buy more stuff when you should be sitting in quiet contemplation creating your latest masterpiece. You already have enough stuff, Saturn in Taurus sister.

Real-World Saturn Return in Taurus Stories

Jessica: Struggling with Codependency

An example of the fixed earthy process of Saturn in Taurus at work during the SR is illustrated by Jessica, a writer and schoolteacher. Money- and relationship-attachment issues became the focus of her SR. She had been dependent upon a very loyal boyfriend for the three years leading up to her SR period. He promised her total security, loy-alty, and financial support, and he even cooked gourmet meals for her. Yet at this time she began to ask herself whether this relationship, beyond the comfy aspects, was in alignment with her true values. She began to think about what really fed her, what really supported her creative voice. If the relationship was truly what she needed, Saturn could deepen the commitment that served her inner growth. However, in this case the relationship was nothing more than a comfort zone wherein her creative voice was dying: she spent all her time with him watching television, repressing her sexual needs, and watching her creative visions wither away in the recesses of her unused imagination. Growing up, Jessica often sacrificed play and creativity to be a loyal pal to her father. She wanted so much to be close with him and find some security in their togetherness that she often found herself attending boxing matches, hanging out in bars, or watching television for hours on end just to sit next to him. He never supported her own creative longings, and instead he spent time teasing her or convincing her to just be one of the guys. This was then reenacted in her relationships with men. As she hit her teens and started to think about college, she realized her father's reckless spending habits on beer and women would not support a solid foundation for her to pursue her dreams. She longed for a father who would sit down with her and go through catalogs of schools, ask about her classes, or even ask to see her grades. She had always been a dutiful character, hyperresponsible when it came to school. She was a straight-A student. However, as her father had never gone beyond a high school education, he had a negative reaction to school and instead valued the grit of hard manual labor. She found no support for her own creative wish to pursue a degree in English literature or creative writing because her father felt this was too impractical and flimsy. As a consequence, she really struggled with guilt when it came to her creativity, her enjoyment, or even doing her own thing. She had learned only to follow her father around like a loyal lapdog and to sacrifice her own play to be in her father's world. She repeated this by letting her boyfriend's world dictate where she spent her time and energy. These were still not her own values.

How does Saturn get his lesson across when he is in Taurus? If not by means of concrete law enforcement, usually the more common manifestations are depression, restrictions, loss, paralysis, stiff joints, hair loss, guilt, fear, or messages from an authority figure in your life. When Jessica's depression became too overwhelming, she had to admit that her relationship was holding her back rather than supporting her growth. By making her boyfriend play Saturn, she felt like a child being grounded. Taurus needs grounding—not creative confinement. Her SR showed her that she had to earn her own values as well as her own money rather than rely on a daddy substitute. At the start of her SR, when she was almost twenty-eight, all these illusions started to break down and she realized there was nothing supportive about this false setup. The structure was too confining because there was a dependency built around it. When she owned her own determination, creative gifts, and ability to make money, she found true freedom for the first time. Now Saturn became a supportive structure in her life versus a burden she felt she must cling to for her survival. She broke up with her boyfriend in the last few months of her SR, when she was just about to turn thirty, and finally began to pursue her dreams. Her writer's block lifted, and she started submitting short stories to literary magazines. Then she began making money from freelance gigs and getting noticed at the local independent paper. This was the true liberation for Jessica. Although there was a fair amount of crisis along the way, the outcome of her SR was just what she'd always wanted. At thirty-one, she is now making it on her own and owning her creative voice.

Macy: Feeding a Wound

Macy's SR brought her food issues to a head. For years she always ate the same exact thing for breakfast, lunch, and dinner. It is common for people with Saturn in Taurus to get into food ruts, wanting to eat the same familiar food items or favorites over and over again. As you can imagine, this can sometimes lead to a health crisis, especially if the choices are not nutritious. In her case, Macy was eating doughnuts every morning with two cups of coffee, fried eggs or a hamburger for lunch, and spaghetti with marinara for dinner. The only variations included substituting pizza for pasta and scones for doughnuts. Obviously, some major food groups were missing from this habitual menu. At the time of her SR, she was suffering from fatigue and low immunity, so she broke down and saw a doctor. She learned that she had severe hypoglycemia and that she was a serious candidate for diabetes. In addition, she had a whole host of other health issues that had to be addressed through dietary changes. As her SR progressed, she made some important changes to her diet, but the fixation with food did not stop. She realized that food was serving as the answer to all of her emotional and creative blocks. Even when she switched to healthier choices, she would often binge on "healthy" junk food like carob bars, wheat-free cookies, and soy milk. Regardless of her choices, at this time she realized how much mental energy went into thinking about and planning out meals. Being an only child, she had spent a great deal of time alone after school while her single mother was working. She remembers that her greatest source of comfort and parenting was eating for hours while watching her TV "parents." She would rush to the refrigerator the minute she felt the loneliness of the empty house while she was waiting for her mother to finally get home from work. Her mother had actually played a very Saturnian, fatherlike role in her life because her parents were divorced when she was four. There had been a lot of pressure in her upbringing to act as the perfect, pleasing girl with strict discipline and high expectations. Her control issues were wrought by a militant mother and were classically enacted and worked out through food. But no one ever thought it was an issue because she never gained any weight until she was much older. She realized at the time of her SR what an important comfort food had become during all phases of her life. Even as a teenager, if she felt rejected by boys she would run home to drown her sorrows in food. Sometimes she would pass up social opportunities just to stay home and binge in the privacy of her room. If there was a choice of entertainment, food would always

Survival Skills for Saturn in Taurus

Sing!

Use your creative voice.

Feed yourself what you deserve.

Let go.

Change.

Empty your junk drawer.

Plant a garden.

Don't hold onto things past their due.

Let go.

Nourish yourself.

Break out of old habits.

Express yourself.

Let go.

And did we mention that you should let go?

take the place of a film, concert, or party. If she felt lonely or depressed, she would often treat herself to a nice meal out or take home her favorite food and comfort herself. The food fixation was furthered when her father came to visit her once a month all in the context of going out to nice restaurants. All of their quality time together seemed to center around fine dining experiences. He would even send her chocolates or candy in the mail to keep their connection. All of these issues really resurfaced during her SR. She had to examine the way food was serving as a surrogate parent, filling creative voids, and masking her deep underlying depression and loneliness from years spent alone with virtually no parenting. When she was twenty-nine, during the last phase of her SR, she found herself abandoning health food and opting for healthy gourmet food while she was dating an older man who loved to dine in the expensive restaurants just as her father did. This grew into a new creative outlet/addiction. As in her childhood, she was compelled to eat and drink away the emotional issues that were being brought up by this new relationship and unconscious need for a parent. By the time of her SR, this had become the central focus of her daily life. From the moment she woke up, she planned the perfect meals at the perfect restaurants. At the end of her SR she woke up one morning and realized that her food addiction was out of control. She was still overweight and exhausted, and she knew that she was medicating herself with food. She realized she never quite felt full or satiated even though she ate at the best restaurants. She decided to finally enter therapy to confront the void that she was trying to fill up with food. As her SR wound down and she turned thirty, she started to get her issues under control. Now she is thirty-four, is at a healthy weight, and knows how to feed herself. She doesn't use food as a weapon to punish herself or as a reward for good behavior. She eats to live rather than living to eat.

Saturn in Taurus Potentials

These are just a few examples of real-life SR scenarios. Other ways to understand the Saturn in Taurus lesson would be to look at circumstances around income, possessions, food, your voice, and honoring your talents. Any obstacles, fears, rules, or setbacks that you experience with these areas of your life are Saturn's way of getting your attention. Some deep structural changes are in process. Remember that you can mine the true gold of your SR when you finally realize this humbling and miraculous truth: you already have a precious gift—you can make other people feel secure. But first you must learn your own true value. If you can get yourself grounded now, you're well on your way to owning the potential of your Saturn placement. Get in touch with the real needs of your body. Make sure that when you feed your belly you are also feeding your soul. Express your needs and unblock your throat chakra. Create beauty within and without. And remember to honor the earth beneath your feet.

Gemini

Gemini needs the newspaper, the radio, magazines, and gossip. Gemini needs to be informed until she trusts her own perceptions. Gemini needs to inquire. Gemini needs to finish her sentence before she changes her mind. Gemini needs to change like the wind. Gemini needs never to grow up. Gemini needs to choose consciously so that she doesn't feel confused. Gemini needs to limit her involvements. Gemini needs constant stimulation. Gemini needs her twin soul. Gemini needs to understand her own mind. Gemini needs to communicate. Gemini needs to take a deep breath. Gemini needs to tell stories and exaggerate every detail. Gemini needs the latest and the next. Gemini needs movement and momentum. Gemini needs to trick and be tricked. Gemini needs to do three things at once. Gemini needs to teach and to learn. Gemini needs to slow down and turn off her mind. Gemini needs to worry, analyze, and hypothesize and finally make light of her experience. Gemini needs to write it all down even if it will all look different tomorrow. Gemini needs to search for her true message.

CHAPTER 3

The Mind

GEMINI

Keywords/Issues:	intelligent, mercurial, quick, wit, communication, thinking, tension of the opposites, duality, versatility, changeable
Ruler:	Mercury
Symbol:	The Twins
Element:	Air
Modality:	Mutable
Opposite:	Sagittarius
Archetype:	The Twins, The Magician
Key Phrase:	I Think
	Gemini rules the lungs, nervous system, upper ribs, collarbones, shoulder blades, and bones in the forearms, wrists, and hands
	Gemini is associated with the third house

The greater the tension, the greater is the potential. Great energy springs from a correspondingly great potential between the opposites.

—CARL JUNG

Is life an eternal pursuit of cutting out the riffraff? Fear of making the right choices? Hearing a twin voice in your head taking back everything you just said? Do you feel like a wishbone being pulled at both ends? Do you question each of your choices every moment? Are you terrified of committing yourself to an ideal, an opinion, or a course of learning? Do you get a rush from a brilliant piece of writing, a joke, or a perfectly crafted conversation? Do you feel there is not enough time in the day even though you are running nonstop from morning to night? Are you devastated that you have to choose among the sixteen thousand things that you want to try in any given week? Do you often feel like Jekyll and Hyde?

When Saturn lands in Gemini at birth, be certain he has a whirl-wind course set up around issues of the mind. He wants to empower you to trust your perceptions and your contradictions and to lose your worrywart tendencies. If you feel as if there is a violent Ping-Pong match in your mind, Saturn will lasso you with his rings. With Saturn in Gemini, life can feel like one big head trip. This might explain why the Buddha is often connected with Gemini energy, because he found enlightenment through the contemplative path. Perhaps finding the wisdom of Saturn here is as simple as finding your own version of a meditation cushion. For Saturn in Gemini women, the right path may be landing here for a breather and letting the constant rumination transform into quiet mindfulness. Saturn will first force you to look at what your mind is filled with. If you have Saturn in Gemini or it is traversing your third house right now, perhaps the following questions are renting too much space in your head:

- Where are you commitment phobic?
- What are your patterns of rationalization or justification to avoid the truth?
- Why are you running? And where or what are you running to? Or from?
- Why are you so afraid of slowing down?
- What do you really want to learn about?
- Which teachers in your life really inspired you?
- Who do you want to be when you grow up?
- What choices would you have made differently?

- What choices would you like to build your life on for the next seven years?
- What aspects of yourself do you deny or reject?
- Where could you use more discrimination?

Mind over Matter

Saturn in Gemini gals seem to either passionately adore their journal or banish it like a bad report card, terrified it might be used as incriminating evidence someday. It could expose the complex workings of their genius minds. (And their deepest emotions.) If you happen to be one of the journal-phobic types, perhaps these questions will inspire you to consider experimenting with the transformative effects of journaling. Not only will it bring you into closer intimacy with yourself, but you will feel Saturn's weight lifting with every word you scribble onto the page. The therapeutic benefit of writing is especially potent for this Saturn placement.

At the time of writing this chapter, Saturn is traversing the constellation of Gemini in the sky (and taunting us as we try to write this). Common issues in our recent astrological counseling sessions have been concentration, focus, and the difficulties around finishing projects—particularly projects calling for reading and writing.

Never-Never Land

OK, let's cut to the chase about this issue of growing up. Here is where Saturn and Gemini have some real problems. Daddy Saturn is clipping your wings as you crash from "never-never land," telling you it's time to grow up. The Saturn in Gemini gal, as if right out of a Toys "R" Us commercial, will vehemently chant, "I don't wanna grow up." Intellectually, she is beyond her years. She is worldly and sophisticated. Yet ask her to do her laundry or get a routine grown-up job, and watch her shriek and run for cover (to the closest magazine stand, most likely). If she feels she loses her freedom or can't fulfill her essential need for variety and new experience, she will likely be crying on the inside. In other words, when she feels Saturn asking for commitment and responsibility, her instinct will be distraction, diversion, or booking the next flight to Panama (Gemini loves to travel).

Just Breathe

Woman, do you ever stop to take a breather? Smoking cigarettes doesn't count; although it may be the only way you will take a deep inhale. Now we know that the Curious George in you will just not let up, but it can also kill the cool cat in you. You simply must see and do it all and then some. Surely "time-out's" were your most dreaded punishment. Saturn invented time-outs, and believe it or not, they could be the miracle cure for you as an adult. Saturn wants you to trust that your mind is so fresh, your insights so sparkling, that you can let a few around-town happenings pass you by and still be the best-informed of the bunch. When you are on fast forward, zipping around collecting data like a census bureau, your nervous system may well be on overdrive. Deep breathing is the quick fix (Gemini's favorite fix), and if it means getting yourself to a yoga class, put down the magazines and go. Whatever calms the mind down—whether taking long, slow walks, counting to three for each inhale and exhale, or hanging upside down until all of the twin-talk empties out—Saturn will support you in spades. Of course the other side of this is that Saturn could inhibit you from really trying new things and trusting new information. This Saturn learns from experience (and often values it even more than academia), so step outside the lines and get a breath of fresh air.

Mastermind

Scrabble champ, Trivial Pursuit mastermind, and crossword puzzle whiz you are sure to be—a smarty-pants who may have studied her brains out and aced every course. And yet, when Saturn and Gemini meet, you may eternally doubt the level of your intelligence. Even if you have a slight learning disability, do not mistake this for having anything to do with your brilliance. Speech difficulty can also be found with this placement when the words struggle to come out clearly. This is also metaphoric for how Saturn in Gemini works when you feel you are stuttering on your real meaning, or not quite hitting the nail on the head. You could feel as if your mind took every detour in town and forgot what the original destination was. Talking in circles is another common defense from having your words used against you. It's a great strategy for seeming as though you are revealing the contents of your mind as you keep everyone chasing after your point while you quietly slip out the back door. The more you dare to speak the words that will reveal your true feelings, the farther you will be on the road to healing any mental traps of isolation or being misunderstood.

Father Issues with Saturn in Gemini

Did your father have his head buried in the newspaper, or was he lost in TV-land? Maybe television was your daddy, or one of the TV sitcom dads became your substitute dad. Maybe your father's idea of communication was grunting or using one-word declaratives to answer complex questions. Chances are that as intelligent as he was, he did not delight in hours of self-disclosure. Probably you experienced him as more of an enigma who used humor or other childlike tactics to divert your attention from probing too deeply. Was he traveling a lot? Chasing knowledge or pursuing myriad adventures instead of being a dad? Or did he just live in his head? Perhaps he also suffered from the Peter Pan syndrome. Did he have an inconsistent or hypocritical parenting style? Was it too easy for you to break the rules and deceive him? Did he treat you more like a sibling than a daughter? Did you find him dodging his responsibilities in favor of more instant gratification? Was he impossible to pin down? On the road? A rambler and a gambler and a sweet-talking ladies' man?

On a positive note, this father may have been a great storyteller. He may have instilled in you the values of getting an education or seeing life as the great opportunity for learning experience. He may have showed you some benefits of staying connected with your youthful spirit or endowed you with great wit. In any case, Saturn the good father wants you to experience life, soak in information like a sponge, and learn, learn, learn everything under the sun until there is nothing left to do but teach it. This Saturn daddy loves structured learning even if done solo without a formal education. Honor your reading and writing time as your most important tools in this life. Let your inner father check up on you to see that you have been doing your homework. Only you know what that is. Chances are the inner Saturn will beg you not to let your brain get soft. Read things that will challenge you. When left to weaker devices, Gemini could have you lost in pop-culture gossip or trashy novels instead of really keeping you on your toes with healthy information. The Curious George in you needs to know what is going on in the world, so staying informed is important for you. Most important, the good father will have you ask yourself the right questions, choose wisely, and deliver your messages on time.

Facing the Saturn Return with Saturn in Gemini

The compromise between Daddy Saturn and the teen-beat Gemini is often a give and take of structure and freedom. For example, one would likely find someone with Saturn in Gemini freelancing. Saturn has no problem with that as long as there is some deeper purpose uniting the various jobs and there is some intention of building. If you feel depressed, guilt-ridden, or burdened at the time of your SR, chances are Saturn and the twins are not in harmony. Don't forget that Saturn has to accommodate and consider both of your twins. It's not an easy task to tame two wild horses veering off in different directions, but this is where the gray area comes in. Where Saturn in Gemini tends to run into difficulties is where there is black-and-white thinking. It's like pitting one side against the other in your mind. Which side is going to win Saturn's approval? He is too wise to take sides, and thus you are left to duke it out in a mental tug-of-war. If you want the alliance of Saturn, he's going to turn up the tension between the opposites until you find the middle path. The wisdom of the gray is where Saturn can step in and be of assistance. In other words, try to avoid the labels "good" versus "bad" or "right" versus "wrong." This will help you to avoid the psychological split and keep the denied evil twin from rearing her ugly head. When intuition goes beyond categorical thinking and finds more subtle channels to inspire the logical mind outside the box, Saturn can serve as disciplined discrimination instead of black-and-white barricades.

Many women, if not already in the therapeutic process, feel an inner urgency to take part in therapy during their SR. This goes doubly true (no pun intended) for Gemini. Yet it brings up one of your greatest fears: intimacy with your own psyche. Perhaps what drives all of that frenzied running around is a deeper fear of someone really getting to know you. At the SR, the need to finally confront this fear of meeting the true self, let alone having real intimacy with another, really comes to a head. You have probably spent most of your life in a kind of denial about deeper issues, until the tension of the SR pulls things apart at the seams. Perhaps you never even asked yourself what you *really* want to do or learn or what you believe deep down. Once Saturn brings the crazy train of busyness to a screeching halt at the SR, the questions are likely to blaze across the screen of your mind. For better or for worse, it is time to commit to finally getting to know the contents of your own mind. Saturn, of course, loves the phrase "settled down." In the Saturn in Gemini girl's case, this settling means confronting any self-deception and rationalization. There can be no more hypocrisy, duality, or avoidance of responsibility.

Saturn applauds the grays but pulls out the whip when he smells fear of commitment. As a teenager it can be cute to have the whimsical, devil-may-care attitude, but evading commitments, appointments, and follow-through as you hit thirty will surely blacklist you from the honorable women of integrity list. Saturn will ask if your words match your actions and if you mean what you say and say what you mean. Integrity is the prime goal of this SR. Are you a woman of your word or a little trickster slipping in and out of responsibility? If you can admit any of the con artist tendencies that you harbor, better to give up the gig when Saturn comes back around. This way you can avoid a slew of Saturnites with your number, ready to reprimand.

An interesting phenomenon that can occur with Saturn placed in Gemini is a fear of writing things down. Some women get over this before their SR, but many report that they fear being exposed through their words; or that someone will find their writing and take them to task for their feelings. There is a fear of commitment, even if it's just committing to some sentences scrawled on the page. Many Saturn in Gemini women don't want to write things down, even to-do lists, because they are afraid that they'll really have to go through with things. Half of these women don't even like to finish their sentences. If they do manage to complete a full thought and are met with agreement, they might retract their opinion before they can be pinned down. Is it fear of commitment or working toward a deeper gray area of thought? The distinction is an important consideration during the SR.

If life feels like a malicious merry-go-round that you just want to get off of, Saturn will throw a cursed mirror in your face and tell you to get brutally honest with yourself. It's either this or spend the next twenty-eight years riding even faster. Your mercurial mind and stunning IQ could best be put to higher pursuits. Your blessed sense of humor will have trouble making light of what has now become crucial and real. Integrity is no longer a luxury to be cultivated at a later date, as you feel the splits in your psyche screaming for attention. It is time to face your shadows. What have you rejected in yourself? The closest clues will be all of the judgments and disdain others bring up in your life. Any statements you feel compelled to make such as "I would never . . ." or "I can't stand such and such" might lead you to those denied aspects of yourself that need more understanding.

Saturn would love us to boil this down to the essential work: What is the message of your life? What is the message you want to spread based on your experience? How can your youthful,

Famous People with Saturn in Gemini/Third House

Joni Mitchell

Martin Scorcese

Orson Welles

Winona Ryder

Paul McCartney

Gwyneth Paltrow

mercurial ways serve you rather than restrict you? How can your intelligence support your growth rather than keep you locked in mental gymnastics and silly crossword puzzles? How can you finally get your head out of the clouds or rather the clouds out of your head? How can you use all of the getaways to find yourself rather than lose yourself?

Real-World Saturn Return in Gemini Stories

Sarah: Getting a Real Education

Sarah grew up in a small town on Long Island. She never finished her undergraduate degree. In high school, she was told over and over that she didn't live up to her potential. Despite this, she was ridiculously smart. Although she rarely studied, she got an almost perfect score on the verbal section of her SATs. Her father was a prestigious psychiatrist in their upper-middle-class community, and although he spent his time listening to and taking care of his clients, he never had time for Sarah. He seemed concerned solely with the idea of Sarah getting into an Ivy League college. He never asked how she felt, only whether she'd joined this or that club at school, or if she finished her entrance essay for the Brown application.

Sarah responded to this by refusing to fill out any applications at all. Instead, she decided to go to community college and got a job at the local Gap. She was miserable. She read everything but the texts assigned by her professors. After a year and a half, she dropped out and moved to the West Coast. There, she lived in Venice Beach, worked at a tattoo shop on the boardwalk, studied many different men, and tried acting. Around the time of her SR, at about the age of twenty-six, Sarah started to get tired of flitting from job to job and man to man. She wanted some stability in her life. She had been estranged from her father since she left home at nineteen, and she decided to write him a long letter. Throughout the years, she'd tried to write him many times, but she'd either give up midstream, crumple up the paper and throw it away, or finish and hide the evidence in her drawer.

Her father didn't respond to her letter, and Sarah was devastated. This is where the Saturn in Gemini woman feels her hurt the hardest: when she does finally say the words, the doors of communication end up slamming in her face. A lifetime of feeling unheard and swallowing her words fostered this negative expectation when she did finally speak. At the SR, an experience such as this can be necessary to stop choking on words. Sarah realized that her feelings about her father were keeping her from pursuing her own intellectual pursuits. There was never any room to develop her own interest in learning for learning's sake. It was all about excelling and getting in to the top school to please her father, killing off any curiosity or will of her own. In other words, her own quest for knowledge was shot down by her father's overshadowing demands to get the status degree. She was never trusted to make her own choices. He never took the time to hear what was on her mind and what her ideas were. Education was a dreadful replacement for love and communication in their relationship, and thus she wanted nothing of it. She started therapy and found great solace in journal process work. About a year after she wrote him the letter, her father finally contacted her. Now Sarah is thirty-two, and she has a relationship with her dad on her own terms. She went back to school at twenty-eight and got into an accelerated B.A./M.A. program. Now she has a great job as a grant writer, and everything that felt scattered and confused feels settled and safe. She is back on track.

Jan: Her Own Mind

When Jan was growing up, she always felt like second fiddle to her older sister, Hillary, two years her senior. She would express her opinion, only to be shot down by her mother, her father, and her sibling. She felt as if nothing she said mattered, so eventually she stopped talking so much. By the time she was five, she became the quiet one, her voice stifled and silenced by her environment.

Even in class, she rarely spoke for fear of sounding stupid. She'd hide at the back of the room, and when she was called on, she would turn fiercely red. She dreaded school because of this and would come up with myriad reasons to be absent much of the time. She was a solid B student, but she felt dumber than a rock. No one knew this though, because sharing her fears was the last thing she would do.

She plodded along this way for years. In college, she met Mike, the man of her dreams. He was a graduate student and a comparative literature scholar, and he knew four languages. She'd had a rather mundane childhood. She grew up with a father that spent his nights lost in the blue glare of the TV set and rarely opened a book, so her new boyfriend seemed perfectly exotic and irrepressibly intriguing. She fell in mad, mad love.

After four years together, Jan's man asked her to marry him. She was ecstatic. There were problems in the relationship, of course, particularly in that Jan often let her feelings go unspoken because she was afraid to rock the perfect little boat she imagined them sailing in. So when he popped the question, she kept her doubts to herself. She was only twenty-six, and even though most of her friends were dating voraciously, she felt ready to settle down. Her fiancé did almost everything for her. He made all the decisions, even down to where they would go for dinner. For Jan, this was just an easy transition from her former family life. They set the date for May of 2000, when Jan would have been exactly twenty-eight and a half. During the two years leading up to the wedding, Jan's mother and sister tried to "help" her with the planning. Instead, they simply took over. Everything from the

Survival Skills for Saturn in Gemini

Write in a journal.

Meditate.

Travel.

Teach.

Remind yourself twenty times a day that you truly are a smarty-pants.

Don't take too much feedback or advice from others.

Trust your gut before the Ping-Pong action starts when you have to make a decision.

Practice focused movement like tai chi or yoga.

Accept that you need a double life of sorts.

Get to know your shadow in therapy; meet Mrs. Hyde.

Catch yourself on exaggerations or truth-stretching maneuvers.

details of her wedding dress to the flowers, the cake, the location of the ceremony, and the honeymoon became the domain of her family. She felt as if her ideas were completely irrelevant. About six months before the wedding, as she sat at the catering hall with her sister finalizing the menu for the big day, she finally lost it. Her sister suggested the filet mignon. Jan wanted the salmon. Out of nowhere, years of repressed rage flew out of Jan. She stood up and screamed at her sister. She told Hillary that she wanted her out of the wedding planning and out of her life. Her sister ran out crying, but Jan felt liberated—guilty, but liberated. Later, when she spoke to her mother, the guilt worsened and she called her sister to apologize. But Hillary didn't offer any further assistance with the wedding, and Jan was glad.

When the wedding arrived, Jan had no small measure of jitters. In fact, she was freaking out completely. She and her fiancé hadn't been getting along for months. As the wedding drew closer, they grew further apart. This is because Jan had finally started to find her voice. She had a heart-to-heart with a friend the week before the wedding, and she realized, finally and painfully, that she wasn't in love with Mike anymore. But how could she not go through with the wedding? She felt as if she had to. What would everyone say? So at first, Jan proceeded, forever the good, quiet child.

She put on her gown and her veil and stood in front of the mirror. Her friend Elizabeth stood by. Then the dam broke, and as she cried, Jan knew that she wouldn't walk down the aisle that day. She called it off, moved out of her boyfriend's apartment, and started a new life. She had to move in with friends for a few months and get a new job. Her old job was barely enough to support her, because Mike had taken care of them both. Her mother wouldn't speak to her for three months. She told Jan that she was crazy. Jan did, indeed, feel crazy. But she knew she had made the right choice, the scariest choice she'd ever made in her life. And for the first time ever, her very own.

Saturn in Gemini Potentials

The Saturn in Gemini lesson will have you constantly on the move, on your toes, and running in two directions at once, so you are likely to take more info and experience into your noggin than are in a Microsoft program. You may earn the reputation of a walking information booth, travel agent, or encyclopedia with your awesome data bank. Not only that, but your choice of words is an entertaining delight and offers tutelage in the fine art of witty communication. This is why Saturn wants to wrestle with you on the communication front. He will have you say what you have to say, and with finesse. You have the potential to be a true messenger.

As you are a tricky little weasel, Saturn gives you the opportunity to use your clever ways constructively. You can steal, cheat, lie, and live a double life if you choose, but when you see how far that gets you, Saturn will raise the bar and ask you to choose your crimes wisely. As the taskmaster, Saturn will eventually bring your true motives to the surface, so discretion is advised. He wants you to put all of your mental prowess to real use in order to build something substantial. It's up to you. Do you want to shoplift or write bestselling novels? Decisions, decisions.

The other great news for Saturn in Gemini women is that you really can stay young and learn to fly. The insatiable curiosity and zippy movement of Gemini cannot help but foster a youthful spirit that seems to flit all over town. At least one of your twin selves might be content to hang out in perpetual adolescence. The key is to use your discrimination because you will have a lot of choices. If Saturn teaches you the maturity of commitment and follow-through, you can use that "double your pleasure" duality. Just pick one thing at a time and do it well, he says. More than any other placement, as a Saturn in Gemini woman, you are offered the opportunity to be killer in more than one trade. Just don't sneak out the back, Jack, and the world can be your own information superhighway.

The bottom line is that you need to trust your own mind and know that you are the sharpest woman in the lot. You can teach all of us exactly what we need to know.

Cancer

Cancer needs nourishment from her roots. Cancer needs sensitivity and gentle care. Cancer needs to take care of her family. Cancer needs coziness, concern, and coddling. Cancer needs her memories and her childhood. Cancer needs to cling to and collect the past. Cancer needs to be mothered. Cancer needs to mother, smother, and nurture her loved ones. Cancer needs her shell, her home, and her protection from the cold. Cancer needs her moods. Cancer needs her security and survival. Cancer needs to be needy and belong. Cancer needs to let herself cry. Cancer needs hurricanes and tidal waves. Cancer needs to sidle up sideways. Cancer needs blankets and pillows. Cancer needs to be taken under your wing. Cancer needs cards and sentiments. Cancer needs moonlight and madness. Cancer needs lunacy and lunatics. Cancer needs nostalgia and collector's items. Cancer needs home.

CHAPTER 4

Home

CANCER

Keywords/Issues:	home, emotions, moods, mother, roots, nurturing, protection, sensitivity, care, sentiment, feeling, childhood, memory, containment
Ruler:	The Moon
Symbol:	The Crab
Element:	Water
Modality:	Cardinal
Opposite:	Capricorn
Archetype:	The High Priestess and The Chariot
Key Phrase:	I Feel
	Cancer rules the breasts and the stomach
	Cancer is associated with the fourth house

The old petrifying mother is like a great lizard lounging in the depths of the unconscious. She wants nothing to change.

—MARION WOODMAN

When Saturn enters Cancer, there really is no place like home. Your lifetime is all about deeply connecting to your inner base, your roots, and your core. The feminine force—the mother, the stepmother, the good and bad witches in your life—is par for the course when sidling up to your life's challenges. Chances are with this placement you would be more comfortable approaching the difficulties sideways, with your protective shell, like the crab that symbolizes Cancer. Delving down into your core also means embracing your many moods and feelings that might change as frequently as the moon. No worries; there is a rhythm to the lunacy that likely colors your roller-coaster emotional life. Do you feel as if life is a never-ending P.M.S. session? Or did you learn at a young age to hold back the waterworks? We hope you have not had to hold in your feelings or become Frosty the Snow Woman to cope with the many moons and moods of Cancer. It is better to think of life as an eternal homage and ritualistic celebration of the many faces of the Goddess as she waxes and wanes within your psyche. With Saturn in Cancer, the life lesson is about finding the nurturing inner mother to see you through the ever-changing cycles and emotional ups and downs of life. Like the good mommy who brings her child inside from the rain to warm her up in the cozy kitchen with a nice hot batch of chocolate chip cookies (or other suitable comfort foods), it is time to play Nestlé Toll-House Mom to your own cold and drenched little girl within. Of course this means a lot more than just stuffing your inner child with comfort food. Let's get to work.

If you were born with Saturn in Cancer or the fourth house, or if Saturn is currently moving through this sector of your chart, you might ask yourself the following questions:

- How does your past have a hold on your present?
- What makes you feel at home?
- What skeletons do you have stored in your basement?
- How do you nurture yourself?
- Where do you need mothering?
- How does your mother have power over you?
- What have you inherited from your mother's side of the family?
- Who are the important female role models in your life?

- What childhood memories are significant in your present?
- Where do your emotions overwhelm you?

Containment and Coziness

When Saturn joins with the womb of feeling that is Cancer, building a strong container for our many moods and emotional states may feel no less impossible than trying to harness a storm. One definite way to control water and stop its rushing movement is to freeze it. This freezing or numbing is often an instinctual response when the emotions become overwhelming with Saturn in the most watery element of Cancer. Just picture dams breaking, floods inundating, and hurricanes raging. Often when our feelings are about to overflow or get dammed up or suppressed, we are sure to encounter a leaking radiator, a toilet backing up, a sink overflowing, or some other literal water issue in the home. The water theme is also likely to be prevalent in our dreams as well when we are about to be inundated with emotional tidal waves in our lives. Maybe you cannot seem to avoid tipping over glasses of water, or you notice people spilling liquid around you or breaking glasses. In some way the psyche will let you know that the feelings are in dire need of flow.

Home Base

The home is symbolic of our emotional base, and water is symbolic of our feeling and instinctual life. The general condition of our home is a great indicator of how we are doing in our inner space. If things look barren, chaotic, or overly organized, see if this does not in some way reflect a similar vibe in your psyche. If the home feels cold or unlived in, perhaps the feeling life is blocked, emotionally frozen, frigid, or just plain cold. This is classically linked with the image of the crab (the symbol of Cancer) with its hard, cold outer shell of protection. Another option is containment or setting limits like a dam to keep the water from flowing out of control. Learning to set emotional boundaries for your feelings without totally freezing them is a delicate balancing act. For example, the infamous female "silent treatment" or "cold shoulder" is the ice-woman approach to boundary setting. This will do very little to keep the feelings flowing. But if you contain your feelings first, before blurting out a nice little soap opera one-liner, you will have the opportunity to make the feelings conscious and constructive.

Moon River

The most refined mode of water is in stillness. Here is where we feel the tranquility of the element and its reflective capacity. Ultimately the lesson is in achieving the containment of the emotions so that they do not overwhelm or drown you. One way is sitting with your feelings versus speeding up and running away from home, so to speak. Saturn's lessons build the emotional container. He will ask you to set limits in the areas where emotions are out of whack. In the areas in which you are frozen, Saturn will ask you to nurture yourself with compassion and define new codes of mothering. The things that your mother said or did to hurt you beg to be replaced with a more sensitive and caring approach. How would you treat your own children's vulnerability and hurt? Saturn will have you put a quick halt to the "no wire hangers ever" style of mothering now, before they start calling you Joan.

Mothering the Unmothered Mother

The emotional imbalances you feel could likely stem from female or mother figures not honoring your feelings or profound sensitivity. Whether they were mean, moody, snappy, self-absorbed, or just ice queens, they probably did not nurture or validate your feelings. Saturn may ask you to create some limits and start to mother yourself in those areas where you lacked positive mothering. He will ask you to have more compassion for yourself by understanding the roots and origins of your pain. Now it is your turn to embrace your sensitivity instead of beating yourself up when you want to cry. Take time to feel things, reminisce, and get comfy and cozy, the way your childhood may never have allowed. It is time to feel secure and wanted in your own skin. It is your time to lovingly nourish yourself in whatever way your wise feminine soul would ask of you. It may depend on your mood of the moment, so give yourself the female prerogative to change your mind.

It may very well be necessary to trace back the lineage on your mother's side of the family to understand the source of the emotional bondage in your present experience. Do some digging into your roots to find out why your mom might lack a certain quality of "mommi-ness" and why her mom may have been such a coldie, too. Get to the origins of any lack of mothering, smothering-mothering, or other glo-rious patterns of dysfunctional mothering that perpetuate the feelings of insecurity you may be wrestling with. Now is the time to really get to the base of any emotional dramas and neediness that may keep you hiding in your shell.

Moody Messages

It is common with this placement to have grown up with a mother who was inconsistent or based her mothering style on the irrational emo-tion of the moment. She may have been overly protective on the one hand but unable to express her feelings or affection to you on the other. There is the possibility that she was too immature to demonstrate much of a maternal quality, and thus as a child you had to protect your-self from feeling totally abandoned by her. Sometimes an external sit-uation creates the barrier to being mothered: this could come through divorce, illness, real abandonment, or death. Again, this pattern might extend to your mother's or father's mother as well as your own par-ents. If this is the case, the void is so great and the need so profound that only those who have lived as motherless daughters can truly understand what it is like.

If you are still in the "I hate my mother" club, despite being way beyond adolescence, or if you realize it is safer to function far away from your mom, you may need to withdraw and get some distance. This is especially true if you feel emotionally slammed by the smallest encounter with her. The maternal relationship may just be a painful reminder of setbacks in general, and you may feel it emotionally imperative to guard against the vulnerability or button pushing that goes on when you are within a five-mile radius of her or any of your family members. At the same time, there are major karmic knots with your mother and family if you are born into the Saturn in Cancer lesson. If a separation helps release resentment and break the negative cycle, then so be it. Just note that Saturn will force you to face the concept of mother in many guises in order to teach you to finally nurture yourself into emotional maturity and out of your protective shell. You will know if you start wanting to throw tantrums with your female friends, female boss, or any other women in your life that your mother issues are out of the bag. Just think of Saturn as a cosmic therapist leading you beyond any agoraphobic tendencies once and for all.

There's No Place Like Home

Another primary issue with the Saturn in Cancer lesson is getting to the bottom of what supports you at your core of cores. Where is your inner home? What foundations have you laid according to the way you've unconsciously inscribed your past experience? What habits have become your floorboards? What limits have become your walls and ceiling? Instincts and habits play a fundamental role in laying foundations that form the base of responses, reactions, and the search for security. This could be quite literal for you and translate into a desire to never leave home. This, of course, begs the question "What is home?" You might prefer to stay in your physical shelter, attached to your mother or some other family member. You might experience addiction and attachment to food, drink, or other nurturing, comforting substances. (Dorothy must have had Saturn in Cancer. And you know what? Judy Garland in fact did!)

An important issue to consider is something that psychologists are always concerned with: early bonding experiences with your mother. Self-help-savvy women around the world know that attachment issues ultimately stem from our earliest experiences of bonding or lack of bonding with the mother. Any weakness or deficient bonding is what is ultimately attributed to compulsive attachment substitutions. This is not news. However, what is finally making its way into our consciousness is our deeper need to connect with the absolute archetypal mother, or Goddess energy, which is a fierce, receptive energy that is totally tuned into the instincts, tuned into the feeling life. Marion Woodman calls this the "conscious feminine."

The Matriarchal Mission

At the time of writing this book, Saturn is fast approaching the sign of Cancer. Thus, by the time this book is published we will be right in the heart of collectively embracing a deep need for healthy, conscious, feminine energy. What in the wilderness does that mean? It means going beyond the outworn stereotypes that still bombard us on billboards and magazine covers. It means going beyond masculine values gone awry as evidenced in the current will to power we see in nearly every television program and magazine. Certainly it goes beyond some of the older, outmoded feminist ideologies, the sort that try to turn women into men. (Caveat: feminism rocks, but it is in constant need of transformation, like everything else.) Certainly it goes beyond our outworn identity as daughters of the patriarchy. It lives as a genuine embodiment of nurturance and nourishment versus caretaking to mask neediness. If you run around smothering other people into dependency on you while neglecting your own emotional needs, you've missed the point. It is the highest level of creative energy or Shakti, the supreme flowing electrical energy that comes from Mother Earth into the soles of our feet and out the top of our head, or crown chakra, according to Hinduism. It goes beyond having a beautiful flowing head of hair or swaying hips.

Homeland Security

Mama mia. It is always a touchy subject to talk about our mother, whether she was the Divine Mother or Cruella Deville. The mother lode is loaded. Just witness the most macho of men lose it the moment someone insults his mother. Yet mother is what our souls starve for way beyond our infancy, and if the connection with mommy did not take place when we were tiny, our needs and fears are all that much greater. The mother wound is primary and at the base of most insecurities. How do we find a home within ourselves where we can rest both in total solitude and in the company of strangers? The Saturn prescription here is strong roots, a solid inner base, security in one's own being, and finally the ability to attend to our own needs like a good mother does. There is, of course, the bigger issue: our society has lost connection with our roots and the solid values of the past—the simplicity of a handwritten letter, quality time with our wise elders, proper nourishment, and so on. This is probably why we face collective crisis and national insecurity is at an all-time high. (Have you noticed that this seems to be the era of homeland security? It's no wonder that movement to protect the homeland was born right before Saturn's most recent trip through the sign of Cancer.) More than any other Saturn lesson (with Capricorn running a close second), Cancer needs to honor the past without being bound by it. It is about keeping the richness and quality of the old ways without becoming frozen in time, outdated, primitive, or archaic.

69

Famous People with Saturn in Cancer/ Fourth House

Mia Farrow

Judy Garland

Goldie Hawn

Madonna

Simone de Beauvoir

Henri Matisse

A lack of nourishment and lack of roots in the good mother, the divine feminine energy, most typically manifests in the form of eating disorders or dependency issues and love addictions often referred to as codependency. If you don't have the ability to tap into your own roots and draw feelings of nourishment and security, this neediness will continue to keep the self-improvement section of Barnes and Noble chock-full for years to come. From this compulsion to that obsession, this addiction to that projection—we will keep coming back to the basic need to feel loved, nourished, protected, and embraced.

At your Saturn Return, you may feel completely orphaned, alone in the world, and abandoned beyond belief. If you are crying rivers, Saturn is working his magic. Not to fear, you are probably crying for the homeless feelings of all of your ancestors. Are you desperate to just take cover in your shell from the hurricanes in your life? Do you criticize yourself for feeling more needy and clingy than ever? Do you understand how much you just need to feel safe? How can you provide the security and rootedness that you have always craved? At the SR, it is time to come in from the cold. The real charity starts at home.

Cleaning Out the Basement

This is also the lesson of descending into the dustiest nether regions of your psyche and your ancestry to see what is really going on at the basement level. What remnants from your lineage are you still attached to like an old chest of drawers stashed somewhere in the cellar of your unconscious? The residue can best be unpacked by going back to your mother's mother's mother's mother's familial line and digging into your father's mother's mother's mother's psychological hand-me-downs. Specifically it is useful to look at any fears, phobias, blocks, and insecurities that may stem from this ancestry. Your family myths and legends are worth checking into if you can get them from the still-living members of your family. If you cannot mine the data of your family history, you can check the irrational fears, phobias, and so on that come up in your own psyche but that do not seem linked with present reality.

The Many-Headed Mother Hydra

The mother's influence as giver of the law which later becomes that nagging voice of guilt or rule making becomes the primary material for the Saturn in Cancer lesson. For better or for worse, this is where we encounter all internalized forms of the good and bad mother. Let's get the difficult stuff out of the way first, as Saturn would have it.

The negative mother classically takes such forms as the devouring mother, the critical mother, the worrywart mother, and the famous guilt-inducing archetypal Jewish mother. Often a blend of these inner mothers rear their heads, especially during the Saturn Return. The negative inner mother heads such as self-reproach, abandonment, or self-destruction cannot be confronted. Receptive energy that can tune into a more subtle voice beneath the negative mother is what is needed. The positive mother energy can soothe these harsher inner lashings of insecurity by gently asking the question: "What do you really need to feel safe and secure enough to put yourself out there in the world?" When you finally find the support from inside, you have slid into home base. Think of this lesson as finally fostering the kind of inner reassurance that would tell you: "You are safe and supported like the earth supports the tree so that the sky is the limit." You might find this a little too New Age and kooky, but Cancer is also that part of us that tends to get loony-tunes. Blame it on the moon. But seriously, lovely ladies, we need this grounding and supportive reassurance from the good inner mother. We need someone to hold our hands and tell us we are OK.

The negative mother who wants nothing to change says things like: "Who do you think you are, trying to do this?" or "Why bother, you are only going to fail" or "You're not good enough, pretty enough, slim enough, perfect enough." These messages come either directly from cruel words from a frustrated or unconscious mother or indirectly by watching the way our mother used such negative mantras to keep her own soul from flourishing. Chances are that this is just symptomatic of a lack of consistent mothering that can be traced back through generations. This is all about the motherless or unmothered daughters of the patriarchy that need to heed the lessons of Saturn and materialize healthy, conscious feminine energy in their bones.

Midnight Endings

Here is where we also meet what Dane Rudhyar has called the "midnight point of the consciousness—that the 'God-experience' can be had." This is to say that Saturn may do some of his best work with and through you at the midnight hour. Thus, paying attention to one's dreams and night-owl instincts, feelings, and habits is of prime importance when working with Saturn in Cancer. You will get some of your best material and insight into who the heck you really are when things come to an end, even at the end of the day. The expression "dark night of the soul" commonly describes profound endings and midnight experiences of darkness in our lives. How we deal with endings of all kinds is indicated by this Saturn sojourn. No doubt endings will affect us in the marrow of our bones with this Saturn, making it essential to process all of the intense feelings involved.

Father Issues with Saturn in Cancer

With this placement, the father is either a real mommy's boy or somehow cut off from his mother, or he was so deprived of warmth of feeling that he might stand as cold as an iceberg. In any case, it is possible that this father may often defer to the mother/wife in the family. He may hide behind her authority or let her do all of the mothering and the fathering while he burrows deeper into his shell. There are likely many emotional wounds and insecurities with this father. He may compensate by having a very nice home or just hide out being a total homebody. His unconsciousness may surface as complete moodiness and P.M.S.–like behaviors that have everyone running for emotional cover from the cranky, crabby atmosphere. This kind of father may often seem like a big baby that you would like to see come out of his shell and take a real stand in the world. Instead he may throw tantrums and tirades when his needs are not met. This may make it more difficult for the woman with this kind of father to foster the security within her to leave her own shell and step out into the world. She too may just feel like throwing tantrums or pouting in a corner when she does not get her needs met in what she feels is the cold, harsh outside world. She may repeat the pattern of the father by dating or working for a mean, moody, Archie Bunker–type of guy. No doubt this is the whiny, needy, touchy, sensitive position of Saturn, so the imperative to make this energy conscious is great, or you may find yourself in crybaby land. Even if one is crying only on the inside, the emotional needs are usually great and need attending to. The "stop the waterworks" approach of the father will only make you feel more unconscious and grouchy. Instead of attending to your feelings you might just snap at the people closest to you or throw a cold shoulder when you are convinced your feelings won't be validated anyway. Better to get clear about what needs nurturing, sensitivity, and unconditional mother love and say no to anything that will interfere with defining your inner security. Delving into and processing the history of mother issues that may have been passed on to you through both parents is also essential during the SR to give you the freedom to uncover your own authentic inner mother. This will keep you alive and conscious in the present moment instead of hauling the inherited dysfunctional mother lode into yet another generation.

Facing the Saturn Return with Saturn in Cancer

At the time of the SR your relationship with your mother is likely to either literally or psychologically come to a head. You may feel you need to distance yourself from her at the time of your SR to stop reacting to her and finally find your own way with the self-care business. If she keeps opening old wounds, you may finally decide to get into some serious introspection and therapy to dig into the past and uproot the source of the pain. Again, this may mean digging into the family history to find out what made it so difficult for your mother to mother you. Or, if you had a smothering mother, why it was so difficult for her to let you live your own life. Where does this dysfunctional mothering madness come from?

Coming Out of Your Shell

At the time of the SR, Saturn will pry you right out of your hiding spot. That's right—no more home girl for you. It is time to face the world and heal the shyness that prevents you from really allowing the feelings to flow in your interaction with others. Either your job or relationship will force you out of the house and into the world. Or you may suddenly feel stir-crazy if you have been hiding out in private for the past twenty-nine years of your life. You will feel a slow, Saturnian pressure that culminates in you emerging from your shell. If you hide behind a snide demeanor or use your great sense of humor to cloak your shyness, Saturn will challenge you and ask you to be real, which could feel like major vulnerability. Yet, in the real world of work and relationships he will call you out. Whether your boss forces you to start making presentations or your partner or friends start demanding to know how you really feel, the hide-and-seek game is coming to an end. It is all to strengthen the woman within. Remember, your Saturn is teamed up with the Goddess energy, so you have some big business to do in terms of letting that divine feminine energy flow in and through every aspect of your life.

Family Affair

Any other familial issues, dysfunction, responsibilities, wars, episodes, and dramas are par for the SR course in Cancer. You could write a miniseries based on all of the unfolding issues that are likely to appear full force at the time of your SR. Family secrets are often revealed. All the karmic family issues are ready and waiting to turn your SR into the soap opera of soap operas. Use this time to firmly establish the role you wish to play in your family. It is also the time to get clear with boundaries and expectations between you and other family members you have a history of trouble with. Define your needs, your feelings, and your limits with the loved ones who are on your last nerve, and things should start to settle a bit.

Real-World Saturn Return in Cancer Stories

Candice: Mommy Dearest

At the time of her SR, Candice had a huge blowup with her mother during a family gathering for her twenty-ninth birthday. At the dinner table, her mother cut off Candice halfway through all of her sentences, told her not to eat certain foods because she was looking heavy, and went on to criticize her choices in friends, clothing, and men. She even criticized her ability as a singer. As the years of frustration had been building up like a pressure cooker, Candice suddenly unleashed a bellowing voice, declaring: "Can you not hear or support anything about ME?! ME, your own daughter! You reject, control, and criticize me constantly. You always undermine my security. I am so sick of letting you hurt my feelings and bringing up more and more insecurities this way . . . just stop it!!! Do you not have one considerate or kind bone in your body?" At that point, she burst out sobbing, and her mother coldly went and locked herself in her own room, with no emotional capacity to be there for her daughter. She could only nurse her own wounds.

Candice had always been a complacent child who suppressed all of her feelings with food or alcohol. Once in a while she threw a tantrum, but it was usually unacknowledged. It was at this moment that she realized she was letting go of a mother lode.

As an only child, Candice had always felt that her mother never heard her or cared about any of her needs. She had grown up mothering herself by stuffing her face with muffins, feeling comforted by television families, and crying herself to sleep. Her mother had also been severely neglected and poorly mothered as a child and was thus still in the role of a needy child instead of a mother. Candice had tried desperately to get her mother's attention, care, and love for years by taking violin lessons, getting straight A's, cleaning the house, even cooking for her mother. Her mother had no loving or nurturing energy left to give Candice at the end of her day working as a nurse. Instead she was always cranky and ornery and snapping at Candice, who decided it was safer to take shelter in her room whenever her mother came home.

Taking shelter became an all-too-familiar way of life for Candice up until her SR at age twenty-nine, when she decided it was time to come out of her shell. The first step was in not only confronting her mother externally but, more important, looking into her own inner mother. The Saturn work required her to separate the negative patterns unconsciously adapted from her mother's lineage from the way she would choose to nurture herself into a secure mode of being. Here she would feel safe enough to go out into the world. She surrendered her nights of eating cake and cookies alone in her apartment with her three cats to going out with her friends and working on coming out of her shell. She also began ritual work with women on the new and full moons. This helped her in myriad ways. Not only did she begin to honor her own connection with nature and the changing influence of the moon, but her newfound connection with the Goddess energy allowed her to open to her feeling life and release the disappointment and anger she was still holding against both parents for not being there for her. This work with women in a sacred, healing, and safe context allowed her to learn the deeper lesson that Saturn wished to teach her about taking responsibility and projecting disappointment and any additional negative traits onto her mother. She needed instead to face these issues within herself.

She also chose to take a break from speaking to her mother or going home for any family gatherings until she was able to process the resentment and unresolved hurt. When she was in contact with her mother she tended to project every disappointment, failure, and need she felt onto what she called "being mothered by a narcissistic five-year-

Survival Skills for Saturn in Cancer

Make your house a home.

Write a letter to your mother even if you never send it.

Cook.

Work with the phases of the moon.

Enter therapy with a female therapist.

Nurture yourself.

Trace back your family history, especially your mother's side.

Join a women's group.

Acquire land or property.

Be a good mother to yourself.

Take yourself to a cozy restaurant or hotel.

Study Wicca or another ecofeminist spiritual path.

old." She decided to dig into her roots to try to understand why her mother was so wounded and unable to play a maternal role to Candice. She needed to understand why her mother was so competitive and cold. By spending more time with her maternal grandmother during her separation from her mother, Candice developed insight and compassion for the weaknesses in her mother's ability to mother. This gave her a resolve to break the pattern before she would have any children. She made a commitment to herself to begin to work on developing a more nurturing and sensitive approach to herself.

Saturn in Cancer Potentials

With the Saturn in Cancer lesson, it is important to honor your feelings even if there is a fear that your neediness could engulf you. It is essential to embrace your vulnerability despite fears that you could be abandoned, criticized, or rejected when you express your need for warmth and affection. If your mother neglected you, smothered you, or both, the need to meaningfully connect with others is the work. Only in allowing the vulnerability that comes with intimacy and dependency can you discover your own inner capacity for caring.

Even if your early domestic scene was filled with deprivation and lack of support, you have the potential to connect with the kind of inner resources that will shelter you. This is your blessing in disguise: true self-reliance and rootedness in the core of your being. You can achieve unshakable security within yourself independent of the changing moods of would-be caretakers. You will realize you never really left Kansas after all, Dorothy. In fact, you will have earned the right to call every place home because you will have unearthed the true wisdom of the saying: "wherever you go, there you are." As soon as you embrace Saturn's affirmation that there was never anything wrong with you, that you are not inadequate or lacking, you will never feel homeless again. Now that you've found your home, it's time to create.

With the hard shell of Cancer, it may feel like you would rather retreat than let your true vulnerability show, but Saturn can assist you in finding strength in your sensitivity. Always honor your immense intuitive strength without second-guessing your instincts. They are likely to be razor sharp, especially at your SR. You have the potential to receive light the way the moon receives hers from the sun. Being so closely connected with the moon, there is so much that you can learn from its waxing and waning cycles. You have the gift to experience this on an inner level without the slightest effort. You are truly tuned in to the ebb and flow of life and can use this to honor the many moods and cycles you are likely to experience. Try not to judge yourself for what feels like moodiness or emotional outbreaks. Just feel whatever you need to feel and Saturn will release his grip.

Learning to nourish yourself from a deep inner level will provide you with a solid foundation that can endure any emotional storm. It may feel especially trying to let go of your past ideas of nourishment such as ties to family, memories, or childhood. Yet, as you connect with the good inner mother, your feminine strength will become more conscious, enabling you to feel secure enough to release old security blankets. Your past heritage will always be a cozy anchor as long as you do not allow yourself to stay mired in memory, regret, or longing for a home that you can never go back to. At the SR, it is all about finding the true inner home that goes with you wherever you go. In this sense, the searching and longing for home can take you back to your inner self, your roots and you can finally settle down to let life nurture you.

Leo

Leo needs the sunshine and the spotlight. Leo needs to shine. Leo needs to create and create and color the town red. Leo needs drama and limelight. Leo needs to dominate, rule, and knock your socks off. Leo needs to show strength. Leo needs pride, dignity, and respect. Leo needs warmth and approval. Leo needs love. Leo needs a flock of admirers and followers. Leo needs to radiate her presence like the sun. Leo needs the applause, the awards, the accolades, and the appreciation. Leo needs to take center stage. Leo needs the royal treatment and the throne. Leo needs to roar. Leo needs to take a gamble and play the high roller. Leo needs a fan club. Leo needs children and laughter. Leo needs to spoil and be spoiled. Leo needs luxury and leisure. Leo needs the love story. Leo needs to be numero uno. Leo needs to be a big kid. Leo needs superstar status. Leo needs your undivided attention.

CHAPTER 5

Creativity

LEO

Keywords/Issues:	strength, courage, bold expression, self-love, the heart, the noble spirit, pride, dignity, show(wo)manship, drama, confidence, the inner child, play, joy, sunshine, love, romance, the actress, recognition, leadership
Ruler:	The Sun
Symbol:	The Lion
Element:	Fire
Modality:	Fixed
Opposite:	Aquarius
Archetype:	The Sun and Strength
Key Phrase:	I Will
	Leo rules the heart and the spine
	Leo is associated with the fifth house

There is comfort in the strength of love;
'Twill make a thing endurable, which else
Would overset the brain or break the heart.

—WILLIAM WORDSWORTH

When Saturn meets with Leo, the noble, creative spirit is burning to take form. The creative voice is yearning to roar. There needs to be a stage, an audience, and applause in at least one arena of life where Leo can display her powers of creative expression. Performance anxiety could keep you watching from the wings until you learn to trust your spontaneous creative impulses without caring a fig for what other people think of you. Even the shyest woman born into the Saturn in Leo lesson needs her share of the limelight, but maybe while no one is looking. Leo is that part of you that demands respect, even if you have too much pride to ask for it. Saturn's reserve may sometimes inhibit you from strutting your stuff like a proud mama lion. But if you give your inner child permission to come out and take a risk, you will be blown away by your own creative potential. No doubt you were born with the sense that you have star potential and yet guilt for wanting any attention. Many women born into this lesson have a sense that they have already been down that star-studded path before, in a past life or otherwise. If your biggest fear is mediocrity, don't fear. Saturn has endowed you with more artistic talent than George W. Bush has talent to abuse the English language.

If you were born with Saturn in Leo or the fifth house, or if he is currently hanging out there, you may ask yourself the following questions:

- Why are you leading the life of a closet or shadow artist?
- What are you dying to create?
- How can you let yourself be a kid again?
- Why do you believe that luck happens only to other people?
- Why does pleasure create so much guilt?
- What risk do you know you need to take?
- When are you going to take your playtime seriously?
- How do you relate to children?
- Why is it so hard to love yourself?
- What does domination mean to you?
- Why is it so important to have the power and control?
- What terrifies you about mediocrity?
- Why do you care so much about what other people think?

The Royal Treatment

The needs to be recognized and to maintain dignity are the areas where Saturn might throw you some challenges. He might pull a few royal carpets out from under you on the stage of life, just to see if you can still hold your head up high. The real test of your lifetime is to have self-assurance without continually checking the applause meter. Especially when the world tells you otherwise, the name of the game is self-love at all costs. Would you still own your royalty if Saturn, posing as the world, took away your title, your throne, and your crown?

I Am Woman, Hear Me Roar

The true power of Leo is strength, courage, and warmth of heart. Of course Saturn can sometimes make you feel more like the cowardly lion. We are talking about the prime of our third chakra (this symbolizes the seat of our will) where we can pack the one-two punch in life in full Technicolor splendor. Saturn wants full-on leadership potential realized when he lands in Leo. He knows you have what it takes to bring others into the sunlight with you, but if you put the cart before the horse, so to speak (major Saturn pet peeve), by doing the John Travolta strut before you have earned your crown, there will be problems.

Perhaps at this point we should get into that touchy subject of ego that sometimes shows up with the queen Leo energy. It is true that regality is your forte, but how do you wear the crown with humility? That is the question. Leo and Saturn together make for one control freak–dominatrix pairing. If you have developed your will and

Famous People with Saturn in Leo/Fifth House

Mae West

David Bowie

Eva Perón

Liberace

David Letterman

Elton John

Ingmar Bergman

paid your dues, Saturn will gladly hoist you up into your rightful position as ringleader, front of the line, top of the charts. Yet with Saturn here you may vacillate between knowing you deserve the accolades and harboring fear or guilt about having any attention showered upon you.

Nobility of Heart

Leo does rule the heart after all, and thus you have the capacity to give and give and splurge until Daddy Saturn takes the T-bird away. On one level, you love to spoil your loved ones and—shh—even yourself when no one is watching. Yet Saturn will throw major guilt trips if limits are not respected or you violate your own rules. If your Saturn is too harsh, you may feel guilty indulging yourself even a bit and play the deprivation game when it comes to luxury or pleasure. One woman quit her art therapy sessions because she found herself actually enjoying the inner work and could not bear the guilt. She did not believe that something that was also joyful could be healing, so she opted for the cold couch of psychoanalysis to avoid the guilt.

Play Hard

Saturn is not antifun, even though legend says otherwise. He simply wants you to structure your playtime and creative work. In fact, if you do that, not only will you waylay the guilt, you will in fact expand your time for fun in the sun, and you might land yourself some brilliant creative work to boot. The Saturn in Leo lesson can make you so talented that you have no time to waste, and Saturn will not let you off the hook. He will be on you to get that creative project started like nobody's business, and if he feels you slacking off, he will throw you under the constraint of an artistic bully-boss just to rustle your ego mane. At some point you'll see that you'd be better off achieving your own creative enterprise. The pride issue will often burn you because deep inside you know you were born to do great artistic things in this world.

The Inner-Child Issue

Oh no, not another silly self-help cliché. (Whoever coined the term "inner child" had to have Saturn in Leo.) Sorry chickies, but when Saturn hangs with Leo, your inner child is likely throwing up a storm of tantrums unless you have a well-stocked creative arsenal at your disposal to appease the Inner Princess. She needs to get dressed up in glamorous costumes, paint, dance, sing, and sew. She needs to do it all, so don't stifle her Picasso potential. Try it, and just watch the sun fade behind black clouds of depression and despair. There is nothing worse than a Saturn in Leo woman who has been denied her canvas, her crayons, or her stage. And hey, let this be a warning to you: if you are playing the stepmother to your own Cinderella, it's time to give up the gig and let her go to the ball. Only the unconscious Saturn has to play evil stepmother, because the conscious Saturn would much prefer to play the role of Fairy Godmother. The message is Saturn all the way: get your lovely arse to the ball, but make sure you also get it home by midnight to finish that painting. Oh how Saturn loves that "midnight hour" time reference. One minute later, and it's all over. Do we ever really get the import of this teaching? One day it will be the absolute, manifest truth, but why wait until then?

Rug Rats

As Leo is connected with creative offspring of all kinds, including your children, the karma you have with your kids will play a role in your own development. Your kids have definitely come here to whip your ego into major shape. Little Saturns they are sure to be. Watch out. Depending on how your own Saturn is doing, they are likely to feel like little Hitlers or little Gandhis. If you have not pleased Saturn and he still needs to play the role of tyrant to get your attention, they will show up in your world to criticize and guilt trip you at every corner and remind you of your failed potential. If you have taken your authority and creative potential lovingly into your own hands, it is likely they will praise you and remind you of how wonderful your accomplishments are and ultimately respect you as supreme role model. No matter what, these kids are likely to be creative dynamos themselves. This is the good news.

The other side is they probably came here to give you hell, raise your consciousness, break your ego in two, and willfully attempt to usurp your authority at every corner. No biggie, just graciously slap a coloring book down in their lap and get back to your own masterpiece. Watch in wonder as the more you do your thing and do it well, truly living up to your creative potential, the more the ferocious little tigers transform into sweet and gentle little kitty cats, as if by the grace of the sun god.

Don't Kid Yourself

Let's talk about your role in this upbringing business. If you still need to be the kid, get all of the attention, and possess all of the control, God have mercy on your children. Saturn in Leo, more than any other lesson, has been traditionally associated with maltreatment of progeny. Of course, this goes double if you were not allowed to be a kid yourself and felt totally ignored, unloved, and unwanted during your childhood. This is one of the hardest cycles to break. How can you learn to love yourself and love your kids without ambivalence if you felt unloved? Forewarned is forearmed, so it is our hope that there is still time for you to create until you feel meaningful self-love, buy lots of parenting books, or maybe just get honest with yourself if you are having a child in place of an unlived creative longing that you need to fulfill first.

If your own inner kid is in good shape and you can allow your children to be children, have center stage, and feel adored, then Saturn will say more power to you. The other side of this placement is that you have what it takes to be a star mother with a most noble warmth of heart and an unparalleled generosity of spirit toward your children. On the other hand, if you are still a needy, greedy Gretchen, be careful that your children are not fading into the background feeling unseen, unloved, and underappreciated for their own unique little selves. One mom with Saturn in Leo was so starved for attention that whenever her kids were watching television, she would dance directly in front of the set blocking the cartoons. What a no-no. This mom should have let herself pursue her dream of becoming a ballet dancer. She would have avoided the need to insinuate herself in front of her children's cartoon hour, embarrassing everyone. The other horror to avoid is fishing for compliments from your kids. Please spare them from having to become the fan club you have always wanted. They will respect and admire you much more if you just get your self-love energy in gear, endowing yourself with enough love and attention to allow their little spontaneous, talented tendencies to shine.

Let the Sun Shine In

Look on the bright side: how bad could it be that your karma is to learn to have fun and express yourself in the most magnanimous and heart-felt way? (Just think, if you were born a little later you would be learning to wash dishes and cut coupons with the Saturn in Virgo ladies. See the next chapter, "Purification.") The only catch here is that Saturn will insist relentlessly that you schedule in playtime and creative time with the same seriousness that you would schedule that appointment to get your taxes done or see your dentist. It sounds so deceptively simple, no? Ah, the agony of making time to create and enjoy yourself—yet you would be surprised how many women with this placement suffer from crazy guilt when they give themselves something they love or indulge in what feels like the luxury of the artistic life. In fact, the guilt can sometimes take on such proportions that they start to believe it feels better to just skip the artistic pursuits altogether. One woman with Saturn in Leo felt so guilt-ridden every time she tried to sign up for the dance class she was dying to take that she opted instead for the treadmill and weights (workout choice of Saturn: metal plus repetition gets him high). The other pitfall to be mindful of with the Saturn in Leo lesson is projecting your own unlived creativity onto your children. There might be the tendency to throw your kids into the overachiever fast-track lane with ballet, tap, jazz, and acrobatics all in one fell swoop.

Hotshot

Saturn wants you in your full-on authoritative glory: power, recognition, awards, and adulation, yes please. This is Queen-Bee Leo we are talking about, and at the Saturn Return it is high time to find your domain to rule, lead, defend, worship, cherish, and empower. You can use the fierce Leo ambition so long as you don't get out of control and become Madonna cum Mussolini toward your followers. There is a tendency to dominate and ultimately get fixed in Leo's stubborn bossy tendency where people might start calling you a control freak behind your puffed-up back. Again, if the ego is in check, you will earn the dignity and respect you so deserve. You came here to accomplish great things, and by devil this Saturn placement will not let you forget it. Saturn in Leo cannot stand to be ignored, overlooked, dishonored, or—worst of all—number two. Leo cannot stand to be common. The will is rock solid with the Saturn in Leo, and you ladies will undergo tremendous challenge if it will win you the respect and hotshot status you so desire. Just make sure all of this die-hard ambition is straight from your heart and not your will to power. Saturn will restrict your high-powered status if your will and your heart are out of sync. Love has got to be the primary motivation and intention in all of your overachiever strivings or you are likely to watch your dreams disappear when Saturn comes for his audit.

Love Is a Four-Letter Word

Hate to break it to your big hearts, ladies, but this Saturn is also the taskmaster when it comes to affairs of the heart. Does Saturn block your ability to scream your love to the sky? There you are with all of this passion and desire for romantic expression, and wham, Saturn whips some metal rings around your heart. If he really needs to get your attention, this could manifest as physical heart problems. You may instinctually hold back expressing the forceful feelings of your love, desire, or affection should Saturn pull one of his insecurity numbers on you as a test. Here we meet yet again the rejection factor; the vulnerability factor; the tired, tired self-doubt factor; and—don't forget—

the oh-so-fun inadequacy trips that Saturn is famous for. You know this little devil just holds you back until you confront these insecurities and banish the word *inadequate* from your vocabulary. Get that self-love trip happening in a genuine and heartfelt way, and Saturn will gladly unleash your gusto and give you away at your wedding. Warmth of heart, generosity, strength, and self-love will break what you were convinced was a bad-luck curse on your love life. This also can't hurt the "oh but when I find the perfect love, and when my love is perfect" complex. Or if you think love and romance are just too much work, get back to working on yourself and that never-ending self-love through self-expression Leo trip, and see if the love/romance department isn't a breeze.

High Roller

Chances are with this Saturn lesson, Vegas is not your idea of a good time. The Leo part of you loves to take bold risks, defy the odds, and come up on top, but prudent, cautious Saturn could put some breaks on the slot machine action coming up triple dollar signs. Don't blame Saturn; he is just asking if you actually believe you deserve to win. Do you treat yourself first class to begin with where this jackpot scenario

Survival Skills for Saturn in Leo

Take an acting class.

Spend time with children.

Take that risk.

Give yourself some glamour.

Spoil yourself and your loved ones.

Take a trip to an art store or an art museum.

Start a regimented program such as *The Artist's Way* or *The Seven Principles of Da Vinci.*

Go first class.

Head up a group or take a leadership position.

Spend more time in the sunshine.

Get regular massages concentrating on your spine and middle back behind your heart.

fits into the main plot of living large? Or do you still sell yourself short and believe good, pleasurable, abundant things happen only to other people? Change your Saturn into a smiling Ed McMahon with the grand-prize sweepstakes check knocking at your door, and watch the odds turn in your favor. Of course this is no substitute for the real-world work of Saturn. You know his brutal requirements are to treat yourself lovingly, create your heart's desire, and live it up a little. If you do this, there needs to be nothing indulgent, irresponsible, or shady about taking a little gamble. We are not advocating taking your life's savings and heading straight to Caesar's to prove your belief in universal prosperity and abundance. Just give up the belief that lucky things happen only to other people.

Father Issues with Saturn in Leo

Your father may very well be the real culprit of your fear to truly express yourself with confidence. He may have done a number of pride-killing tricks to squash your delicate young creative yearnings. He may have in fact showed up like a creative antichrist to tease and taunt you whenever you tried to make a bold move or take an artistic risk in your life. This would all depend on how well he lived out his own creative potential and self-expression. Was he noble and regal, or did he strut his stuff around the house like a pompous ruler? Maybe he was apt to steal your thunder, tirelessly demanding center stage. Did he embarrass you by putting on a show or grand display of eccentricity in public? No doubt this man demanded loads of respect, earned or not. This is the king of the "stroke my ego" daddies. Let's hope your dad was head honcho of something to quell that fiery macho mania, or you probably felt like you were living with Napoléon.

As with the Aries and Sagittarius Saturns, there is the issue of temper here. Insult the pride or dignity of this father, and watch him beat his chest like King Kong. A life with this man should be titled "feed me to the lions." Just don't marry another wildcat, unless you have always dreamed of joining the circus. If you have partnered with a firebrand, just get in the damn ring with the whip and work it all out in your own time. Saturn is patient.

If your Saturn karma is in good shape, this father could have been the perfect master of his artistic craft and paved the way for you to do great things. He may have served as a most noble mentor to nurture your creative gifts. Certainly he was put in your life to help you take risks and master your will. If he gave it to you boot-camp style— "stomach in, chest up, shoulders back"—kindly take the discipline and discard the barking orders. If he said things to bolster your self-esteem, inhale those deeply into your heart every single day. But if there were words to undermine your self-confidence, be sure to mark them out with a big red *X*, and start throwing out that garbage pronto. Let all of your creations be a grand celebration of the new self-love slogans or at least a powerful mutation of the old ball breakers.

Facing the Saturn Return with Saturn in Leo

Are you going to take your creative gifts seriously? This is the burning question when you approach thirty. If you are ahead of the game and know you came here to create something special, then Saturn will ask for the proof or push you to the next level. Saturn likes you to feel you are always at the beginning so you will avoid complacency or slacker syndrome. This is the humble position, where there is always more to do and to learn. Saturn has to keep you on your toes creatively. If you are still in the closet-artist phase, he will ask you to get real and sched-ule in time to fulfill these creative urges. Wherever you find yourself at the Saturn Return, whatever you have been working on in terms of your self-expression will be brought to the forefront. Delay no longer with your plan to manifest your heart's true calling. If you do, Saturn could throw you down a dark hole of mediocrity and meaninglessness at the SR. The path to hell is laid with brilliant creations left uncreated.

If you have yet to encounter the brilliant *The Artist's Way* workbook by Julia Cameron, find it; this program was practically made for you. It is in fact our recommended SR supplementary workbook of choice for Saturn in Leo ladies. It's all about reconnecting with your inner child and your inner artist and confronting all of the blocks and resist-ance that may have held you back until now. Saturn will love the struc-ture involved in recovering your fullest creative potential.

At the SR you may feel as if Saturn just checked you into the land of the loveless. If it is the self-love lesson he wants you to get, you may feel like he just gobbled up your fan club, your admirers, your doting friends, and your amours. You may feel as if you are the one taking all of the love and yet still needing more reassurance that you are special and loved. This complex, needing to always be the special one, is a hard nut to crack, but with Saturn on the case at the SR, he will demand you possess your special self if it means socking you in the heart first. Maybe your boyfriend dumped you, your show got canceled, your art was rejected, or you did not get the promotion. Whatever the form, just know there is a loving message behind the seeming devastation that appears to have stripped your life of all glamour and love. Saturn is simply saying: "The gig is up and now it's high time you love yourself! Stop looking outside for the pats on the back, the kisses, and the compliments." There will be no more fishing for compliments at the SR because if this needy performance does not hit its final run, Saturn will empty out the auditorium. The end. He would rather have you take a long hard look at yourself in the dressing room mirror—sans the costume, the makeup, the role—and see if you really love yourself. This is the drag-queen drama coming to its finale: with the wigs and makeup stripped off, who is really there? Do you love her?

Real-World Saturn Return in Leo Stories

Josie: Starving Artist

Josie was a typical Saturn in Leo multitalented star. When she was young she would dance, choreograph shows for her neighborhood, draw, sing, and sew. Before her innocent stargazing spirit was subdued by adult censorship, rejection, and criticism, she would naturally create and sing her little heart out at a moment's notice. She would often pretend to make commercials while looking in the bathroom mirror as if she were the spokeswoman for her favorite toiletries. After repeatedly having her spirit beaten down by her father, who told her she was making a spectacle of herself, a light went out. She took all of her Leo energy that was muffled at home and started overcompensating by bossing around all of her friends. She became the leader of the pack and basically called all of the shots. At home she felt unloved, unappreciated, and unseen. To make up for this she would quietly control her group of friends. She would often pit them against each other to prove their adoration of her. She subjected her friends to a lot of tests to prove their love and devotion to her. This never seemed to make up for the lack of love she felt at home. She was even popular—a little heartbreaker—with the guys. She just played with everyone's heart to remain in control. Deep down she never felt she was really lovable, and she was afraid that if she dropped the act and let anyone really get to know her, they would just end up rejecting her like her father had. She felt comfortable only when she was acting her part and bossing others around. It gave her a false sense of esteem.

In her college years, instead of pursuing her true love of drama and the arts, she took her need for control and respect and enrolled in the business track. Her creative spirit was dying. She would let her spirit out only when she was alone, drunk, or with a few very trusted friends with whom she could really let her true self loose. Other than that, she was under the spell of wanting to impress her father by doing what he respected rather than following the call of her own heart. Even though she always received the highest marks, her father could barely be bothered to bat an eyelash. He was so wrapped up in his own world of architecture that he neglected his daughter's need for attention. She started to feel frustrated that she had sacrificed her true passion to pursue what she thought would finally win her father's love and respect. Saturn's teaching was creeping up on her. She had abandoned her own inner creative spirit.

It was not until the heart of her SR right before her thirtieth birthday that the bomb really went off in her head. She was miserably working for a tyrannical boss at a top firm in Chicago crunching numbers, using about 2 percent of her creative talents. The boss happened to perfectly replicate the treatment her father had given her. She felt either as if she had been run over by a Mack truck because of his insults and lack of heart or so infuriated by the audacity and size of his ego that she was burning with rage and resentment. The day before her thirtieth birthday she collapsed in the office from chest pain. She was rushed to the hospital, and doctors found that she had a virus in the lining of her heart. The lack of love and neglect of her heart had manifested itself physically. Her father never even came to visit her in the hospital.

From her first day of recovery, she made a pact with herself to get back into loving environments that supported her true creative longings. She decided to start singing one night a week to give her soul some expression, and she took an acting class one night a week. She gave up the corporate world with the abusive boss and traded it in for a lower-paying but more creative job where she was treated with respect and had room to develop her ideas. Three years later, she was auditioning for theater and commercial work. With that Leo-like perseverance and strength of will she landed her first real theater job within six months of first auditioning. From there she went on to produce shows, teach singing lessons, and even start a small line of silk scarves she designed.

Saturn in Leo Potentials

The brilliance of this Saturn placement is a regal quality and loyalty in your character, which make you absolutely lovable. When you love, your warmth spreads like the warmth of a beautiful summer day. You have a way of defining elegance and flair for the dramatic like no other Saturn placement. You possess showmanship beyond measure. You have a strength and magnetism found in the greatest leaders. You have the opportunity to embody the strength of Eva Perón and the meow of Mae West.

Of all the Saturn placements, you have the most potential to shine in any number of creative domains. Many women with this lesson devote their life to developing their artistic skills. You have the ability to experience the world of art and creation with true discipline and reverence. If you value your time and know that it is precious, use it to develop your artistic longings and start creating now; you have no idea how far your multiple talents can take you. If there is any hesitation, it could only hold you back and block your show. Is it fear of looking silly or being judged as incompetent or lacking talent? If you harness the courage to confront your critics within and without, let your noble spirit soar, and offer no apologies, you will have become the sun.

Virgo

Virgo needs to refine and purify every last detail. Virgo needs to sort, sift, and surrender. Virgo needs to bring like things together. Virgo needs to maximize the minimal. Virgo needs the toothbrush, the comb, and the floss. Virgo needs to be the humble healer and the sweetest servant. Virgo needs to be the helper and the one who shows the way. Virgo needs the recipe, the map, and the directions. Virgo needs to break it down to put it back together again. Virgo needs lists, laundry, and lightness of being. Virgo needs the please and thank-you and the napkins. Virgo needs the cleanup and the empty closet and cupboard. Virgo needs to dot the i's and cross the t's. Virgo needs the medicine cabinet and the breath mints. Virgo needs to analyze, agonize, and organize to keep the messy and the chaotic at bay. Virgo needs white linen. Virgo needs worry and work, work, work. Virgo needs vitamins and Handi Wipes. Virgo needs precision and practicality. Virgo needs ritual, rites of passage, and regimen. Virgo needs synthesizing and integration. Virgo needs virtue and virginity. Virgo needs to be all alone to see that she is all one.

Purification

VIRGO

Keywords/Issues:	ritual, purification, simplicity, service, solitude, magic, cleanliness, work, health, practical, details, perfectionism, analysis, synthesis, health
Ruler:	Mercury
Symbol:	The Virgin
Element:	Earth
Modality:	Mutable
Opposite:	Pisces
Archetype:	The Hermit
Key Phrase:	I Analyze
	Virgo rules the intestines
	Virgo is associated with the sixth house

The woman who is virgin, one-in-herself, does what she does—not because of any desire to please, not to be liked, or to be approved, even by herself; not because of any desire to gain power over another . . . but because what she does is true.

—ESTHER HARDING

Through practices of purification, service, and solitude as the sieve, Saturn brings us into the bare-bones confrontation of ourselves when we are all alone. Saturn's teaching through the archetype of the Virgin is where we encounter what Marion Woodman has called: "She who is who she is because that is what she is." In this work, we must clean out our closets, empty our drawers, and meticulously figure out where to put all of the psychological loose change.

Cutting through all of the superfluous melodramas of life, we are stripped to our simple truths. If we are to discover what we are in our most refined essence, we have to attend to all of the details of who we are not. We will be called to attend to the nuts and bolts of our work, our selves, and our lives. In the face of a world that supports extroverted "doing," how do we find a necessary introverted "being" state? Saturn will teach you to have the courage to stand on your own.

If you were born with Saturn in Virgo or in the sixth house, or if he is currently residing there, you might want to ask yourself the following questions:

- What does it mean to be all alone?
- What is solitude versus loneliness?
- What does it mean to be truly of service?
- What do you worry about?
- What makes you feel healthy?
- What is the perfect daily ritual or schedule?
- What are your particular, picky, perfectionist propensities?
- What are your rules and rhythms around work?
- How many different ways can a problem be analyzed?
- How can you get things in your life down to a science of simplicity?

On a very practical level, this lesson is where scheduling and day-to-day details can drive one over the edge of neurosis. Do you worry, chew your nails, and pull your hair out in the hopes that obsessive-compulsive schedule making can make it all go away? Do you feel a maid and a personal assistant are the keys to survival? With this Saturn lesson, it is likely you could suffer from the "not enough time" syndrome. Putting off daily grind tasks is also likely to be your great spiritual challenge, thanks to the greatest perfectionist complex in the zodiac. Do endless to-do lists buried under piles of the undone and unfinished plague your every waking moment? Do you get a high from rearranging your stuff in hopes of finding the perfect working system of minimalism and cleanliness? Do you envy the friends that seem to know how to put like things together so effortlessly?

It is very likely that in this Saturn realm you could get into binge and purge, obsessive-compulsive disorder behaviors around many daily tasks. You could either avoid your personal appearance and show up less than fresh for everything or go hog-wild hitting every manicure station and grooming salon in a five-mile radius. Same with work, as Saturn in Virgo is famous for the workaholic syndrome. The question is, what are you really trying to purge by burning the candle at both ends?

Serving Yourself

What about this deeper need for service? Do you work only out of safety, comfort, or routine? Or does work fulfill a greater yearning to really offer your Goddess-given talents to synthesize and analyze until you have come up with meaning and placement for every thought flower available to mankind? With the Saturn in Virgo lesson, there can also be a fear of the projected weight and responsibility or lack of glamour that come from certain service/bordering on slavery positions. Then again, we spoke to many women going through this lesson who dreamt of such simple (a Virgo key word) and satisfying service positions.

As Virgo is also associated with those that you employ and people who are of service to you, it is common to find the typical Saturnian delays, frustrations, and disappointments in the help arena. Many women with such a placement report comical to tragic stories with regard to employees or hired help. Perhaps Saturn's teaching speaks to the age-old idiom: "If you want something done right, you have to do it yourself." Many a righteous woman born into this Saturn lesson has had to take the plunger into her own hand because the plumber is likely to screw it up.

Blades of Grass

Nitty-gritty, nuts-and-bolts work and service issues can polarize into their opposite fantasy—escapism and glamour galore. This Saturn tutelage loves to rip the veil of illusions out from under you like a red carpet being replaced by cement floor and a to-do list. Depending on Saturn's strength in your consciousness, you may either shun all forms of living on Fantasy Island or hop on the mental Concorde straight to la-la land whenever the piles of laundry and dishes get closer to the ceiling. The issue here is to find the gold in the seemingly dreary coal of daily existence. Like many enlightenment enthusiasts that exhort us to find the meaning of the universe by studying a blade of grass or baking a loaf of bread, Saturn loves anchoring you firmly into focus on the finest details. Marion Woodman calls this mining of your own psyche in bare-bones (Saturn loves this phrase) terms: "kitchen work." Interestingly enough, addiction is often healed by attention to alternative daily rituals and work to keep the idle hands out of trouble. "The devil [Saturn] makes work for idle hands" is a great motto of this Saturn lesson. The implication is that in our flight for the sublime and the transcendent, the law of the opposites will usually crash land us back into the world of feeding the dog, showering, and getting back to work.

Embodiment

There must be some way to bring some glamour into this practical arena of life. The key is in the word *embodiment*. Women born into this lesson can submerge themselves in all of the glamour, dreams, schemes, whims, and fancies their hearts desire, just so long as they are willing and able to put in the hard work required to make them materialize. They must be crafted into form and made useful for Daddy Saturn to get involved in a positive way.

Virgoan rhyme and reason is much like following a recipe, which is why many a woman with this Saturn setup are often found fleeing from the kitchen even after trying to follow *Cooking for Dummies*, unless, of course, this issue of orderly protocol has been mastered and no longer feels like oppression. Then you can open the Betty Crocker manual with ease. Saturn's intention is to teach us about the rewards of going step by step with such measured tasks. Should we decide to make up our own rules about how to best dice an onion or bake a cookie, Saturn will be there to support us as long as we honor the Virgo lessons of precision and attention to detail. In Indian spiritual philosophy this principle is known as *Shradda*. This helps the spiritual practitioner to remain in the present moment. It's interesting that in its purest state, this painstaking attention to detail (like not dropping one grain of rice on the floor) is, ultimately, love. If you think about that inseparable connection between our longing for work and our longing for spirit, you will realize how intertwined and complementary these two aspects of our psyche in fact are. The work and detailed focus brings into being such divine qualities as patience, faith, and compassion, which cannot manifest without grounding in the present moment. This is why if you embark on the spiritual path expecting glamour, you are usually brought to a screaming halt. It may seem oh-so fabulous to meditate on beautiful swirls of chakra colors in Bali, to become a raw foodist, or to go on a change-your-life cruise to the ancient islands to bring you enlightenment. But watch yourself reel in horror when confronted with the Mr. Miyagi/Karate Kid "wax on, wax off" approach. The hard-core Saturn Master knows that handing you a broom and a dustpan or offering you an opportunity to volunteer at a homeless shelter is the real way to get you to the goal. Think of all the money you will save knowing that your true evolution as a whole soul can happen without even leaving your linen closet. Saturn will throw major kudos at you for getting outside of yourself and helping, being of true service. This is the best antidepressant for this Saturn pairing—namely, get to work and help somebody out. If you're still feeling a little blue, hit the health-food store.

One of Saturn's favorite measuring sticks is the usefulness scale, and this goes double when he is found hanging out with Ms. Practical Pants (Virgo). It's one thing to really clean out the sock drawer or arrange your books in alphabetical order when things start to feel out of control, but beware of the usefulness and priority requirements of Saturn. Are you avoiding or delaying something that could be of an even greater service to you or another? Beware of some of the cunning pitfalls that are likely to try to keep the dillydallying intact: reshuffling, worrying, and obsessing to name just a few procrastination techniques of the pro perfectionists. Saturn might have to crack down the hard way to show

Famous People with Saturn in Virgo/Sixth House

Anna Freud

Paul Klee

Dalai Lama

Rainer Maria Rilke

Thomas Moore

Ralph Waldo Emerson

Henry Miller

Julie Andrews

Meryl Streep

us that things will never be perfect and thus there is no time more perfect than the present to start the work. Forget about the dishes that are undone or the shirt that really needs to be tailored before you can get back to that unfinished task. Saturn was not even going to fall for our own ploy to delay the writing of this chapter until we had perfectly read, sorted, and analyzed any and all pertinent research pertaining to it. Quality, of course, is of Saturn's domain. No question, he wants only the best, but he also reminds us that the path to hell is laid with good intentions. He's all about the crystallized form, not the realm of possibilities. Saturn demands hard copy when he lands in Virgo. Stop your fussing and fretting, he would say, and get down to work.

PalmPilot Princess

What is this search for the perfect daily schedule? Astrologer Caroline Casey reminds us that Saturn is all about finding our own internal rhythm and authority. If we don't, we'll likely be handed a 9-to-5 schedule by some external Saturn figure. But what if we were left to find our own perfect daily schedule and rituals? What time would we get up? When would we eat? Even further, when would be our day off? What time would we go to bed? How many hours would we work? When would we play? Perhaps you have already created your own daily regimen without any imposition from external influences, but chances are that if this lesson applies to you then you are still working it out on some level. One woman struggling with this issue would take out her schedule every Sunday night with stars in her eyes as she sought to create the perfect plan for the new week.

Saturn reminds us that what we spend our time doing is the true measure of what we value. If you value health food, working out at the gym, and doing wheat grass shots but spend most of your time working in a smoke-filled bar wolfing down French fries, Saturn is likely to crack the "major discrepancy" whip. You will feel it in your health or in the depression resulting from a job that is totally out of whack with your values.

Father Issues with Saturn in Virgo

When Saturn teams up with discerning Virgo energies, it could land you a father that scrutinizes the details of your work life like Martha Stewart on speed. Dirt under your fingernails, my dear? A messy drawer? Bedsheets not folded just so? A Saturn in Virgo kind of father has supersonic flaw radar. What's that minuscule scratch on your car door? You worked only ten hours today? How can you live with all of those empty shopping bags under your sink? Did you take care of x, y, and z? Your father may especially seem like a walking voice-over reminder of your own neurotic tendencies. This father is not likely to let you forget about the mundane details of your life, and he may never feel that you work hard enough despite glaring signs of burnout. Of course not, because he more than likely burns the candle at both ends himself.

Did your father impart his wonderful worrywart tendencies? It is likely that phone calls or conversations with this man feel like neurotic interrogation sessions. If there is anything that can make this father worry, it is likely to show up in his health, so reassure the both of you. You may have grown up watching your father transform into the incredible Mr. Clean, spending hours scrubbing, polishing, and arranging. "Neat freak" is probably an understatement with this sort of father. This is where the issues of perfection and criticism come into play. He was likely your first Saturn teacher to take a fine-toothed comb to you and your life, either instilling in you the perfectionist complex of champions or creating a powerful antiorganization movement. Either way, you can see why this arena of your life may have become such a struggle.

If your father is too rooted in the mundane and the practical, you may have felt guilty charting your own way. Perhaps he was a workaholic without a cause and taught you that as long as you work hard and make a buck, you're on the right track. Likely, he is in a service position of some sort, but the important issue is whether this service is fulfilling his real calling or just allowing him to worship at the altar of the dollar bill.

The good news with this kind of father is the responsibility factor. This tends to be a dad with good work ethics and a sense of duty toward his dependents, especially his pets (he might spoil them even more than he spoils you). This kind of father is likely to be reliable and show up on time when you really need his help (you just may have to wait until everything has been put in its right place and he has finished washing and polishing his car for the twelfth time). You may have inherited this sense of responsibility. It could feel dreadful for you to let anyone down, especially in a work context. If not, you will come face-to-face with your dependents and work duties during your SR. The guilt and self-reprimanding will be relentless in this case. This father is also likely to instill good, plain common sense and simple values. The practical things in life—from trips to the hardware store to coupon cutting—are his specialty. If you want the simple truth, this is the man to give it to you. He may also have the best flair for the art of minimalism so that you learn the true value of the "less is more" or "keep it simple" approach to your life.

Facing the Saturn Return with Saturn in Virgo

At the SR, all of the little messy corners of your life are likely to be blown up until the chaos is front and center, staring you right in the face. Forget spring cleaning; try a major overhaul of the recessed clutter of the past twenty-seven years. Your inner finicky Felix is about to streamline your inner slobby Oscar. Hang on, because Saturn is going to scrub the floors, take out the trash, and give you a new paint job to boot. He wants your former cluttered life to look and feel like a Zen palace when he's finished. You can start now by organizing the loose change in your kitchen drawers and throwing out the junk and the dead wood.

Not Enough Time in the Day

As work and daily scheduling are prime issues at this SR, any weaknesses in your scheduling abilities are sure to land you in a Time Management for Dummies course. Your life will probably bring you scheduling demands if you don't have an efficient way of working or rituals that ease your workload. You could find yourself approaching a serious overload, a burnout phase. If your work, no matter how full of service, is out of alignment with your values, your body could start loud protests at the SR through chronic fatigue, exhaustion, burnout, or anxiety attacks. There could actually be a major health crisis. It is common for women living through this lesson to feel that they have been slaves to their work and scramble for their emancipation papers as soon as they feel Saturn approaching.

The Hermitage

At the SR you may feel any unmet needs for solitude or time to find your own inner guiding light—a neurotic's must. If you are overloaded and drowning in details of your daily grind, at the SR you are best advised to head for your cave of choice. Get some quiet, alone time fast before you start unconsciously sabotaging relationships that block you from having enough time to reconnect with your own inner direction. Saturn will remind you that before you can truly be of service to anyone else in your life, you need to get out of the worrywart, list-making mode. Have you been making up lists during your meditation time? Excuse me, ma'am, do you not take time to meditate? At the SR it is going to be meditation or Xanax. At the SR, Saturn will put the pressure on to get your world so simplified that you can step away from it for a while to catch some much-needed alone time. If things are too chaotic and disorganized to take a retreat, Saturn might slap some kind of physical ailment or restriction on you to ensure some quiet alone time and simplification of your workaholic tendencies. Taking care of your physical health through proper diet, exercise, mental attitude, and so on is of the essence at your SR with Virgo, so be mindful and clean up any sloppy habits.

Real-World Saturn Return in Virgo Stories

Sarah: The Workaholic

In the middle of her Saturn Return, at age twenty-eight, Sarah was in a serious relationship with a man who really valued spending time together in the evenings and on weekends. Before this relationship, she had been single and into herself in true Virgo-hermit style. Putting her Virgo analytical abilities to good service, she was working as a life coach to help others find focus and effective use of time and scheduling in their daily lives. Ironically enough, these were all of the things she struggled with.

At the time of her SR, she would see up to ten clients a day, often working late into the evening hours and cutting into any available time she would have with her boyfriend. She was also working to the detriment of her health. As all good Virgo/Saturn combinations would have it, she had ideally designed the perfect day to include meditation, exercise, work, and play, but the reality was that she had fallen off the beam by hiding out in her excessive client load. The Saturn problem had even taken on the physical form of blocking her intestines. Her digestion was a mess. She had no energy and felt as if rigor mortis was setting into her body.

Years had gone by with neglected plans to get her daily life into more balance and health. She was caught in a habitual pattern of working until she dropped followed by crashing into unconsciousness through sleep, movies, or wine to escape the drudgery. This insanity became unbearable when Saturn, disguised as her rigid boyfriend, played the Virgo role of critic and went to town on every nook and cranny of her chaotic lifestyle. The combination of his reprimanding her and throwing his own perfectly simple, balanced life in her face drove her over the edge.

This Saturn boyfriend was a poster child for meaningful work, healthful eating, relaxation, creativity, and meditation. All the elements were somehow woven into his daily schedule in perfect integration. This was a major mirror of her Saturn in Virgo issues. Her boyfriend threatened to end the relationship with her if she did not make changes in her life.

She of course had vowed to cut back, slow down, focus on the priorities, and deal with her own time-management issues many times. Yet, her partner demanded action and concrete proof right away, and with enough consistency that he could believe her. She, of course, feeling the weight of Saturn's threat, experienced her boyfriend as a rigid, complaining, tyrannical father figure. She had a choice. She could heed Saturn's call and integrate the changes into her life, or she could fight and have Saturn, in the form of her current lover, dump her as she proudly defended her chaotic lifestyle. Of course she could not make the changes simply to please an external source such as her boyfriend, and she knew it. She realized her only real attraction to him was the way he had mastered his daily schedule. Other than that, he embodied a lot of cranky character traits and severe incompatibilities that were not worth reconciling. When she finally got this, she took matters into her own hands, just the way Saturn likes it. She decided she would not let this control-freak boyfriend dictate her time line to get her life in order. Instead, she would honor and appreciate the fact that her obsessive-compulsive boyfriend was simply an

Survival Skills for Saturn in Virgo

Get some nutritional counseling.

Look into courses on organization and time management.

Work on simplicity in every area of your life.

Take silent retreats.

Clean, clean, clean, and organize.

Practice to strengthen your concentration and attention to detail.

Follow recipes; don't just throw it all in the pot.

Cut out workaholic behaviors.

Get yourself a consistent daily schedule.

indication of her own inner struggle. She ended the relationship and took a retreat to a very structured boot camp–like ashram to internalize daily rhythm, structure, and discipline into her life. When she returned, she struggled but made great strides to get balance back into her life. She woke up earlier, meditated, and created a reasonable working schedule with her clients. She set limits on how many hours she would work each day and made sure to take the time to eat healthier foods to improve her digestion. She spent the next few years of her SR single to internalize the inner father. Within a year after her SR, she met a fabulous, hard-working guy—one without a stick up his ass. He was still grounded but possessed the same love of spontaneity and adventure that she had. She felt much new freedom now that her lover no longer had to play the tyrant/critic to whip her life into shape.

Jane: Service Reigns Supreme

At the time of her SR, Jane had been working as an office manager for a very ornery psychiatrist. She was in charge of all the details such as insurance billing and patient records. She was very industrious and loyal, working long hours for little pay. It was not until the time of her SR that she started to realize that this work was not allowing her to pursue her true calling for service. In fact, this true calling was so close to her that it could have hit her over the head and she may not have noticed. She read many books relating to psychology and healing. Deep in her heart, she really wanted to be a psychiatrist, but up until this time she had just been blindly living in the shadow of her own dream. Her Saturn was grumbling at her all day in the form of the cranky psychiatrist to get her to wake up and realize he was unhappy stuck beneath loads of paperwork. Her potential had been completely neglected. At the time of her SR she had to confront what had been keeping her from pursuing her own career calling—medicine and healing.

At the time of her SR, she started arriving later and later to work for the psychiatrist. She was unconsciously putting her job in jeopardy, perhaps because she no longer wanted to spend her time working this way. Her resistances to showing up on time or working effectively were major red flags. Her values and her life were highly out of alignment. The grumpy psychiatrist embodied the harsher side of Saturn when he confronted her by stating: "Maybe you really do not want this job! Your negligent behavior is showing me that this is too low a priority for you, and since you obviously have more important things preventing you from fulfilling your duty here, I might have to ask you to leave."

As many of us feel in the midst of a confrontation with Saturn, she was filled with fear and doubt. Yet, at the same time there was an inkling that maybe this was the only way to own her potential, scary as it was. She could choose to stay under the tyrannical thumb of her boss and shrink back from taking possession of her own inner Saturn. Or she could face her fears, step up to the plate, and structure a step-by-step plan to achieve her true call for service in the form of medicine. She decided to pursue medical school the following fall.

Saturn in Virgo Potentials

The archetype of the virgin, or "she who is who she is because that is what she is," is the highest potential of this lesson—to be whole within yourself, to be all one instead of alone. Saturn at this stage will take you into a hard-core detoxification from worry, obsessiveness, excessive ordering, criticism, and perfectionist tendencies. He can bring you closer to simplicity, humility, service, and integration. Work becomes a symbol for service and how you attend to the details of your life. Health and personal organization are also symbolic of how well you are doing with the synthesis of mind and body issues. Inner chaos of the mind will surely appear in the arenas of work or health. Ritual and regularity are key elements to keeping this area of your psyche healthy. They show you how to pay attention to your own need for daily structure and rhythm and regularity with your work, your health, and the way you focus and finish all of your tasks. Saturn can teach you to develop your skills and truly be of service to all of those who are dependent on you, including your small furry friends. Finally, this is a key area where Saturn reminds you of one of his A-list no-nos: wasting time.

Libra

Libra needs partnership. Libra needs balance. Libra needs sweetness and light. Libra needs charm. Libra needs air. Libra needs to be fair. Libra needs art. Libra needs her scales. Libra needs smarts. Libra needs her equal mate. Libra needs kindness. Libra needs grace. Libra needs her shadow. Libra needs to beautify. Libra needs to go out and look pretty. Libra needs ideals and ideas to live by. Libra needs justice. Libra needs to get noticed. Libra needs approval. Libra needs parties. Libra needs to be the belle of the ball. Libra needs equality. Libra needs her other half.

The Other

LIBRA

Keywords/Issues:	harmony, companionship, negotiation, beauty, romance
Ruler:	Venus
Symbol:	The Scales
Element:	Air
Modality:	Cardinal
Opposite:	Aries
Archetype:	Justice
Key Phrase:	I Balance
	Libra rules the kidneys and lower back
	Libra is associated with the seventh house

We cannot look to another human being to complete our soul process. The inner marriage is a divine marriage, the outer marriage a human one.

—MARION WOODMAN

Libra is the sign of the "other." When Saturn lands here, relationships often feel like a battleground. Your most valuable lessons come to you through the lens of your intimate relationships. (We're not just talking about romantic partnerships here, but they do get a strong emphasis with Saturn in Libra. All one-to-one relationships fall under this lesson.) If you were born with Saturn in Libra, you've probably been dancing this tango from the beginning. You may experience much in the way of delays, blocks, and disappointments in your relationships. You probably understand the true meaning of loneliness. Liz Greene, esteemed astrologer, says of this placement: "We seek in others what we are not able to express consciously in ourselves; and we also hate in others what we are not able to express." This is the search for companionship in a nutshell: we are trying to make our singular existence whole by adding another half. But with Saturn poised here, the struggle is formidable and often painful. All the stock is usually placed into the investment called "partnership." Often the search for the truth—that is, the inner marriage—is neglected in favor of filling your life with joint ventures.

If you were born with your Saturn in the seventh house or Libra, or if Saturn is making his way into this segment of your chart, you might ask yourself the following, perhaps uncomfortable, questions:

- Do you feel guilty for feeling incomplete?
- Do you hide out in your relationships?
- Are you terrified of true commitment?
- Do you seek status and power in a partner?
- Are you searching for a husband/father combination?
- Do you feel marriage/partnership is the ultimate quest of your life?
- Are you afraid of being alone?
- Do you let your partner take care of you?
- Do you take care of your partner? Too much?
- Do you feel constantly judged?
- Do you use relationships as your mirror?
- Do you compare yourself too much with others?
- Do you let others set the rules for you?

Union is the essence of the Libran search for its Holy Grail. It cannot imagine a life alone. Libra is the sign of the scales, always searching for the perfect elixir that will provide it with the balance it seeks. Libra feels a lack of equilibrium intensely, much like the princess and the pea, when anything is out of balance. Balance is the eternal, archetypal quest. That is why all of the partner's quirks and foibles are internalized by those born under the Saturn in Libra lesson. Your paramour better live up to your expectations, or at least pretend to. If not, you will likely notice and make your irritation known. (Or maybe you'll internalize it and bite the inside of your cheek raw with rage.) You often can't tell where you end and your partner begins. This is why your lover must have hair that glistens and shines, possess a vocabulary that is matchless and grand, and know when to reach out for your hand at the right moments. If your partner fails you, you fail yourself. Your cohort—more than merely a reflection of you—is you. This is why your mate can't screw up. When he or she makes a mistake, all of your own mistakes are magnified.

And this is often true for even those Saturn in Libra women that haven't totally committed. The reality is that you may have an inability to commit that is more profound than that of any of your friends, even if they see you as the one who always has a partner. This is because you can't commit to someone else until you commit to yourself. Cheesy self-help books tell us that we can't love others until we love ourselves. Cliché as it sounds, it's true.

You may feel as if you've spent too much of your life alone. But until after your SR is finished, it's likely the perfect relationship will remain elusive. People born with their sun in Libra are known to be fickle, so those with Saturn here tend to feel painfully inadequate when it comes to making wise decisions about their love lives. You may not be so great at picking winners and instead opt for the first available partners. This could be because of your fear of being alone forever. Because marriage and partnership are so built into your life plan, if you haven't snagged a mate yet, you may harbor nightmares of spinsterhood. We are here to let you know that that's not necessary.

Shadow Dancing

"Shadow dancing" is a concept coined by revolutionary astrologer Edwin Steinbrecher. It addresses the way that relationships bring us into a dance with our own shadow side.

In the Greek myth of Psyche and Eros, Eros insisted that Psyche make love to him in the dark. When Saturn is in Libra, we tend to live out this myth: we give our love in the dark, afraid to look at its true face. The urgent longing to know the Other is often equal to our fear and refusal to know ourselves. Heavy-duty stuff. In order to help you to wrap your gorgeous brain around the dense, mysterious universe of the psyche, we need to introduce some rather complex concepts. Please note that we offer only a very, very simplified deconstruction of stuff that fills entire books. The famous Swiss psychiatrist and contemporary of Freud, Carl Jung, believed that we have within us what he called the "shadow." This is all the unconscious baggage that we have repressed, the muck, and the disowned parts of ourselves. The shadow represents what we do not want to look at. This includes all of the things we have decided (as early as age seven) are "not me." (When Saturn is in Libra, one tends to find exact replicas of the shadow and to date and/or marry them.)

This brings us to the concept of "anima/animus." In women, the *anima*, is considered to be the archetypal masculine force within us. It often defines our relationship with the men in our lives. In women, the anima is shaped, in part, by our relationship to our father or strong masculine role models in our life. The people that we're attracted to tell us a lot about the state of our anima. According to Jung, men and women possess both the anima and animus. When these two forces are in disharmony (they almost always are), we feel split or torn apart by inner conflict. Jung said: "The soul cannot exist without its other side, which is always found in a 'You.' Wholeness is a combination of I and You, and these show themselves to be parts of a transcendent unity whose nature can only be grasped symbolically." When you can get these two forces into balance, you can achieve what Jungians call the "inner marriage." For Saturn in Libra ladies, this is the ultimate quest.

Next we come to "projection." Projection is played out like an endless game of bad-relationship badminton when Saturn meets Libra. You may find yourself enduring many volleys when it comes to getting along with others. It works like this: our psyches have many blind spots, and we often go shooting in the dark for a target we hope will bring us back to ourselves. The truth is we really have no idea of who we are in our entirety. Although we get glimpses in all of our one-to-one relationships. We are on the path of individuation, the attempt to put the broken Humpty Dumpty pieces of our Selves together again, so we can finally stop the childish "not me" game. In our attempt to do this, we often fall into the trap of blaming the people around us for the garbage we don't want to own, or just the issues we fail to recognize as our own. So we project our disowned feelings onto them. If you wake up in a bad mood because of an unpleasant dream, you might roll over and decide that your boyfriend's snoring is so unbearable that it is ruining your life. If he doesn't get the adenoid surgery next week, you will leave him straightaway. It's all his fault. This prevents you from having to look at the back story, to examine your own psyche. We often ascribe the feelings of our inner world onto an external being—boyfriend, mother, father, sibling, friend, teacher, boss—you name it, they are all screens for our myriad projections. When you are mired in these projections without understanding their origin, you can experience what feels like enormous relationship tension, which you're likely to blame on the other person. "God, what the hell is wrong with him? Why does HE keep doing that?" you ask yourself and anyone within listening distance, too. Saturn in Libra women sometimes fail to recognize that issues we have with others are only symbolic representations of

Famous People with Saturn in Libra/Seventh House

Martha Graham

Jane Austen

Sting

Diana Ross

Warren Beatty

Norman Mailer

Queen Elizabeth I

our own inner issues. When you are mired in the Saturn in Libra lesson, you often find yourself looking for the ideal mate, the perfect match, and everyone might seem to be a disappointment. And no matter what the relationship, even if it's not a romantic one, you are likely to experience this kind of unconscious projection madness when Saturn is in your Libran sector.

Static Cling

This Saturn in Libra lesson is the most famous for maintaining a long-dead relationship way past its demise, just for the sake of companionship. The "real estate relationship" is common here, where you've signed a lease with someone and can't leave because neither of you are able or willing to move out. Or you may cling to comfort when you know you aren't in love and know you'll never truly fall for the person you're with. Perhaps you'll stay with a partner who is much older than you are, for security purposes. Saturn here likes to marry the father figure. Sometimes women born into this lesson marry for money. (Sorry for the "ouch" if this is you.) You may even convince yourself that true love will blossom in the wake of a gorgeous wedding with all the trimmings and a closet full of fancy gifts. As you gaze upon the china that came courtesy of your "commitment," you hope that the pangs in your heart will reveal themselves romantically. If you've come this far and you're still feeling something other than true love, we hate to break it to you that it's not very likely to appear. You may need to give up the gig and look at what really ties you to your partner.

I Went to the Land of Love and All I Got Was This Lousy T-Shirt

In love, we seek to lose ourselves in the dreamy narcotic haze of romance, of sex, of our reflection in the eyes of the beloved. This impetus toward drowning is fairly universal. There is a biological urge toward this kind of merging, this longing to make the halved self whole. This is why we so often offer ourselves up on the altar of love, not content to simply offer parts and to share, as an equal, in relationships. The typical dysfunction all of us have experienced is that we give too much. That cheesy book was right: women *do* love too much. And when Saturn meets Libra, this hackneyed idea is the word of god. In order to avoid dealing with inner Saturnian darkness, the woman experiencing this lesson will mummify herself in the swaddling cloths of her relationship until she can't see who she is anymore. Maybe she has never known. Maybe she has consistently given all of herself away so much so that she never figured it out. There is a shadow pull between independence—a fierce, girl-in-the-wild side—and a complete dependence on others that borders on the compulsive. The Saturn in Libra lesson concerns learning how to think, be, and do for yourself first, so that you can eventually be comfortable in a mutually beneficial and egalitarian relationship.

The Good Girl

Libra is nothing if not *nice*. Diplomacy and fairness are hallmarks of the Libran condition, and when Saturn lands here he can force you into a corner of falsified sweetness, of doing anything to be liked. You may have always been the one who smiled despite hardship, who bit your tongue in the face of anger. Libra despises confrontation. The Saturn in Libra lesson teaches you that being the good girl all the time can have dire consequences. The longer you perpetuate your own myth, the longer you will harbor ulcer-inducing resentments against all those who you oblige without complaint. There might be a line around the block filled with folks that aim to take advantage of your compliant ways. But we offer you this bit of wisdom: if you refuse to be a doormat, they'll turn around and go home. And you'll be OK without them.

Father Issues with Saturn in Libra

If you were born into the Saturn in Libra lesson, your dad may have been the type of guy that waffled a lot. Maybe his head was always in the clouds. Maybe he deferred to your mom all the time. Saturn in

Libra women often grow up with dads who do whatever it takes to keep everything calm and balanced. Your mom may have worn the pants, just because your father dreaded putting them on himself. He may not have seemed very dadlike, perhaps a little feminized. He could have been totally noncommittal, too. He may have tested every option, weighing everything on his mental scales to the point of causing utter frustration to you and the rest of your family. You may have looked to him to play the traditional role of father, the decision maker, but with your Saturn placed here, it's likely that your father lacked a fundamental ability to come to firm conclusions. An essential problem with this is that you, as the woman born into the Saturn in Libra lesson, have probably always needed an authority figure to make your decisions for you. The message your father may have sent you could well inform your choice of malleable mates.

Did your dad judge you unfairly? Despite possible passivity on your dad's part, he may have given you some serious complexes. Even if his judgments weren't verbalized, you probably felt them powerfully. You may have needed to play the role of good girl with him all the time because you were terrified of disappointing him. Did you feel as if you couldn't argue with him? Did he repress his anger? Did you learn from him that conflict should be avoided at all costs? Did you always have the feeling that the balance he strove to create was a great facade to cover the real issues in your parents' marriage? Did your folks stay together for years even though it was clear that they shouldn't be together? Fathers of daughters born into the Saturn in Libra lesson often teach them that the integrity of relationships supercedes inner needs.

On the other hand, your dad may have been fair, diplomatic, and tactful. He could have been the type of guy that oozed charm and intelligence, sweeping rooms of men and women alike off of their feet. He may have had excellent aesthetics and lovely taste. Did he love art and beauty? Maybe he taught you a lot about this realm. Perhaps he seemed to possess a rare balance between his masculine and feminine halves. Did he have a good relationship to his own mom? Was he committed to her? He could have taught you a lot about temperance in relationships, too. If his own Saturn was healthy, he may have taught you the value of honoring all of your relationships. He could have been extremely considerate of all of the people around him.

Facing the Saturn Return with Saturn in Libra

When the Saturn in Libra lady faces her SR, she might very well start obsessing over wedding gowns. The grand march toward the altar can become the focus, and if there are any prospects around, they better duck fast, for you have probably trained your laser beam betrothal detector on them. You want the security of a permanent bond more now than almost ever before, and you are probably willing to put important things aside to attain your perfect, storybook wedding. Even if your potential partner is flawed, and flawed he most certainly is (as we all are), you are likely to lasso him in at this time until he brings you the ring. Once he does, it's all easy breathing, right? For those enmeshed in the Saturn in Libra lesson, no such break is likely.

A more likely scenario is a breakup. If you're involved in a long-term relationship, when you hit the SR, your partner's true face is apt to be visible to you, and you won't be able to hide from it anymore. The frisson-laden confrontation with the animus happens at the SR. "Oh my god, I married an alien!" might be your refrain at this time. Choose your B-movie title, because the monster is likely to come out of the closet at the SR, and he's not pretty. It could even be that you live out the better-received *Sleeping with the Enemy*. But the scariest moment of this horror flick comes when you look in the mirror and see the monster's head resting on your very own sweet, soft neck. By the end of your SR, you will recognize his face as your own. You are both Beauty *and* the Beast.

No More Ms. Nice Gal

We may sound a little harsh, but it is only to get you to do Saturn's work. When Saturn knocks on the Libran door to wedded bliss at the SR, he is asking only that you stop projecting your qualities, good and bad, onto the mysterious force called the Other. You must own your shadow now, or you could spend the next thirty years fighting with him about the dirty dishes in the sink. Saturn offers you the opportunity to scrub the kitchen pure of anything illegitimate. If you do your work now, you will be able to see yourself, authentic and beautiful, in the sheer and shiny reflective gleam of the projection-free countertop, clear as day.

During the SR, this refusal to recognize the differences between ourselves and others can become the crux of a crisis. You are likely to find yourself investigating the minutiae of your relationships like never before. And once the SR begins, you may find that someone in your life is always playing the role of Saturn, restricting you, criticizing you like a disappointed father. It could be your romantic partner, but not necessarily. It might be a parent, a friend, or even a client. This phenomenon can occur with anyone with whom you are bound in the tie of a relationship. The war of the roses can start the minute you sign a contract, take on a roommate, or say "I do."

Private Eyes Are Watching Me

One of the most powerful manifestations of the Saturn in Libra lesson is the critical lens that seems to land on you from all sources—any you would term "the Other." Your romantic partner, roommate, parents, teachers, boss, even an underling—you experience heavy criticism from almost everyone. It could be from a complete stranger in a café, but at the SR, the censure that comes to you feels like the most important report card that's ever graced your mailbox. If your first inclination is to hide it under the couch cushions, know that this is exactly the behavior that Saturn will kick your pretty arse for. Take it out of the envelope and look carefully at the red ink. There is vital information there. Not that the criticism you perceive from others necessarily reflects reality. It is probably inflated and almost ridiculous, writ large and bloated, like a neon sign that you can't seem to detach from the marquee of your being. When you meet someone, even for the first time, you might project a severe criticism about the way you look, the way you talk, the way you act. Your style of dress and mannerisms are easy targets. Your intelligence, too. Whatever comes up, look at it closely. Why are you so sensitive about this part of yourself? Who criticized you about it when you were young and impressionable? Who made you believe you were so fundamentally lacking something?

Breaking Up Is Hard to Do

One thing Saturn will do for you during this particular lesson is break down any relationship that is no longer serving you. If you've tolerated living in a love-limbo for too long, the SR will often end it. If you've been holding on too tightly to someone, despite the fact that you know the person is not right for you, a crisis event at the SR can cause a needed breakup. It might be painful to endure the good-byes, the moving out, the cleaning up—but letting go of a security blanket partner is one of the most liberating acts of Saturn's lesson in Libra. If your relationship is anything less than the real thing, Saturn is apt to swoop in and enforce a needed separation. Getting dumped sucks. But whether you're the dumper or the dumpee, this is where you let go and finally find yourself.

Problems with your partner are apt to come into sharp focus at the SR, and you may find that you're no longer capable of sweeping issues under the rug. There are often domestic battles, and they can hurt . . . a lot. You are

Survival Skills for Saturn in Libra

Take yourself out on a date.

Indulge in art and beauty.

Realize it's OK to be alone.

Make your own decisions. Stick to them.

Don't compare yourself to anyone else—you're competing only against yourself.

Walk the balance beam.

Don't judge yourself.

Collaborate.

Know yourself before you waste time getting to know anyone else.

likely to feel as if your partner has put you under the lens of a very high-powered microscope, and the criticism might be pretty intense. If you forget to take out the trash when it's your turn or show up late with the wrong gift, watch out for the arrival of a massive bunker buster. Domestic bliss is not a likely scenario at the SR. If your lover screws up, you probably won't take it easy, either.

Fence-Sitting

When Saturn marches through Libra at the SR, it is likely that you will have to effectively shit or get off the pot in many important areas of your life. You will probably be forced to make decisions that you would prefer to avoid. Libra is well known to be diplomatic, but when Saturn lands here, the diplomacy often turns into confusion—there is a powerful fear of decision making under this influence. If you've been able to skate by thus far despite your inability to commit to any established side of an argument, ideal, job, person, or restaurant choice, at the SR, something is apt to happen that will force you to make a choice. The beauty of this is that you can learn to make choices with ease now and to stick to the decisions you make. No more waffling for you. You'll probably become quite content with the choices you make and suffer little regret when you look back on them.

Real-World Saturn Return in Libra Stories

Lucy: It's a Nice Day for a White Wedding

When Lucy was growing up, she dreamed endlessly of meeting her perfect mate. She fantasized about weddings and replayed her princess scenario in her head over and over again. Even when she was very young, she knew exactly what her gown would look like and the color of her bridesmaids' dresses. It was her primary daydream.

Her dad doted on her and seemed to idolize her. She had a classic Electra complex—she even asked him directly if they would get married when she was five. She turned into a little flirting machine the moment she entered school. She wanted every boy to like her, even if she didn't like him back. She had her first boyfriend when she was seven. And she announced this fact over and over again to anyone that would listen. She was proud and firm, even as a child, in the belief that a relationship was evidence of her place in the world.

It went on this way for years. In high school, she had two major boyfriends, and she couldn't stand the idea of being dateless. She broke up with her first boyfriend only when she had the next one lined up, so that she wouldn't have to spend any time without a relationship. She hid out with her boyfriend and had few female friends. She defined herself by his likes and dislikes, his hopes and dreams, and even his schedule. Eventually this built up a strong resentment in her, but she stayed with him until college. She admits now that this was totally out of fear of being alone. She fantasized about marrying him early on. But sophomore year of college she met Jared, a knight in shining armor, or at least she thought so at first. They started dating in October and were engaged by May of the following year. For the first few months, Lucy was in heaven. He represented everything she wanted: he was charming, smart, soon to be successful, from a good family, and witty. After a few months, though, some of his flaws began to poke through the surface. He was always late, he wasn't a very good listener, he didn't support her artistic interests, and he was a little bit self-absorbed. But he was always *there*. As the months progressed and it became clear that he was going to ask for her hand, she felt alternately terrified and gleeful. She felt that all the things that had been plaguing her—her fear and indecision and inability to commit to a major at college—would come together once she and Jared were engaged.

They started fighting every day, almost as soon as he gave her the ring. Although the night he asked her seemed perfect, its aftermath was horrid. All of his less-than-wonderful qualities began to irk her to the point of exhaustion. She stayed up some nights in bed next to him, unable to sleep because everything felt wrong, but she was unable to break it off. They were married a year after they met, in a beautiful ceremony on his father's estate, she looking as gorgeous as she'd dreamed, and he as handsome as she fantasized about. But inside, something was missing for her. She was only twenty-two years old.

As her marriage progressed, her desperation worsened. He seemed not to notice how unhappy she was. She would nag, but she would rarely yell, even in moments when she wanted to go ballistic. She would instead turn her anger inward. But she'd seethe, and she started grinding her teeth at night, unable to deal with the feelings that were coming up in her psyche. Instead the emotions went straight into her body and began to destroy her. She started getting urinary tract infections, and their sex life suffered as a result. (Libra rules the kidneys, so it's no wonder that her psychological condition manifested in this area of her body.) By the time her SR started, she knew that her marriage was in tatters, and she wanted out. But still, she was afraid to be alone, having had a constant stream of boyfriends since she was seven. They tried counseling, to no avail. She went to see a therapist on her own and had to face the fact that the relationship had to end. Still she held on, enduring a sexless, loveless relationship for an entire year longer, because they shared an apartment and a bank account. One thing that Jared did well was provide for her. She'd allowed herself to slack and was unemployed when her marriage began to fail in earnest. Leaving him was even scarier because of her financial situation. She knew she'd have to give up a comfortable lifestyle and a reliable, if unappealing, security blanket. The process unfolded slowly, but waking up began to get harder every day. She would turn around in bed and cry silently with her back to her husband. She felt trapped and terrified. When she started having nightmares in which Jared appeared as a monster that would jump out of the closet and strangle her, she knew that she had no choice but to leave. She spent a week in a nonfunctioning state, unable to call friends or do errands. At the end of the week, in total despair, she knew what she had to do.

One evening, before Jared returned home from work, Lucy took all the strength she had and, through her tears, packed a suitcase. She was twenty-nine and a half years old and leaving her entire life behind her. She went to stay at a friend's house and told Jared the next day that she'd be seeking a divorce. He allowed her to have it without a fight, but she suffered deep loneliness and was forced, for the first time in her life, to really look at herself. Without a constant companion around to project off of, Lucy spent time with herself, a lot of time. She put herself back together, slowly, and figured out what she wanted to do with her life. She had abandoned ideas of attending law school when she married him, and she decided to apply before her SR was through. The idea of dating remained repellent for some time, although she wanted to get dressed up and taken out to dinner more than anything. Even though friends offered to set her up, she refused to compromise.

She wanted to be with someone whom she truly respected. There would be no more default men in her life. Once she made this commitment to herself, her self-concept improved radically. Now, at thirty-five, she is practicing law and in a loving and committed relationship with a man whom she is truly in love with. It didn't take long at all for Saturn to act on Lucy's pledge to honor her lesson.

Saturn in Libra Potentials

One of the reasons this is such a hard lesson is that our society puts a tremendous amount of pressure on us to find the perfect mate. Add that to the karmic burden of a lifelong quest for companionship, and you get a lesson that is not so easily learned. One of the hardest issues with Saturn in Libra is that our culture has taught us that if we haven't found our life partner by the time we're thirty, we're through. Old maids we will be. This sentence has gotten a little less harsh in the past few years, and single women in their thirties have even been celebrated a bit. (Thank you, Sarah Jessica Parker.) But still, the ache exists in us, and for Saturn in Libra ladies, it's a little more profound.

But there's no need to despair, because your Saturn placement is actually a gift. One you face your SR and take a good, long look at your real needs, it's almost a certainty that you'll find someone who can meet you and love you on your terms. If you make the inner marriage work first, your life partnership can feel truly storybook.

You have the potential to become truly balanced and to have healthy relationships with everyone in your life. You can actually integrate your shadow, something that those who don't face this lesson aren't usually able to do. You can get a great deal of joy from socializing and have amazing business partnerships, too. Partnerships of all sorts can be fantastic for you. This is because once you go through Saturn's Libran lesson, you are equipped to collaborate and cooperate without projecting your stuff onto anyone else. This is rare, and folks will appreciate you for it. The number one reason people go into therapy is trouble in relationships. If you pay attention to Saturn's wisdom, you're likely to experience a lifetime of healthy ones. Rock on, sister.

Scorpio

Scorpio needs the deepest darkness. Scorpio needs desire incarnate. Scorpio needs to fight to the death. Scorpio needs you to die for her. Scorpio needs pure passion. Scorpio needs sex, sex, and more sex. Scorpio needs the underworld. Scorpio needs to get to the bottom and burrow there. Scorpio needs you to go to hell and back for her. Scorpio needs black leather and lace. Scorpio needs to sting when she is attacked. Scorpio needs to shed her skin. Scorpio needs to rise again. Scorpio needs the pits of despair. Scorpio needs the mystery. Scorpio needs to penetrate. Scorpio needs revenge. Scorpio needs to plumb the depths. Scorpio needs to be reborn.

CHAPTER 8

Transformation

SCORPIO

Keywords/Issues:	regeneration, resourcefulness, secrecy, power, magnetism, healing, disintegration, catharsis
Ruler:	Pluto/Mars
Symbol:	The Scorpion, the Eagle, and the Phoenix
Element:	Water
Modality:	Fixed
Opposite:	Taurus
Archetype:	Death
Key Phrase:	I Desire
	Scorpio rules the genitals and the generative system
	Scorpio is associated with the eighth house

Possession is one with loss.

—DANTE

The lessons learned when Saturn meets Scorpio are profound ones. They engender a special relationship to the concept of mortality. Scorpio is the sign of death, of metamorphosis, of letting go, finally and forever. When Saturn meets the underworld, you are likely to be desperately chilled by the very idea of letting things go. Look in the dusty corners of your psychic home. Are they cluttered with sheaves of dross? Is there a necklace of albatrosses around your neck, dear? Like women encountering the lessons of Saturn in Taurus, those ensconced in the hard-knocks school of Saturn in Scorpio tend to despise change. Taurus and Scorpio are polar opposites of the zodiac and are deeply linked by their shadow relationship. When you encounter the Saturn in Taurus lesson, we ask you to look first in the dusty corners of your home, not necessarily your psyche. The clinging is of a less material nature when Saturn makes its home in Scorpio. The Saturn in Scorpio lesson is probably the most difficult to understand of all. When we come to face the Saturn in Scorpio lesson, we are dealing with the tricky triumvirate of sex, death, and other people's money. At first consideration, these issues may seem unrelated, but in fact they are just as complex as you are. Not to worry, Saturn will ground these esoteric mysteries while Scorpio uncovers their deepest message to save you in your darkest moments. Your life with Saturn is all about the phoenix rising from the ashes. And like the song says, "I Will Survive" can become your mantra.

If you were born with Saturn in Scorpio or the eighth house, the following questions may have plagued you since you first learned the fine art of self-torture, at a ripe, young age:

- Where are you afraid of change?
- What do you need to finally surrender?
- What secrets do you hide even from yourself?
- Where would you like to go deeper in your life?
- What obsessions or fixations have a hold on you?
- Do you have any self-destructive tendencies?
- Are you possessive with your favorite people and things?

- Do you struggle with jealousy?
- Where do you need control?
- Do you fear delving into the depths of your psyche?
- What is your relationship to your sexuality? Do you use it for power or control?
- What do you owe to others?
- Do you play a bit of S&M in your relationships?
- What are your legacies? Do they control you?
- How are you tied into other people's money?
- What are your debts?

Sex, Death, and Other People's Money

According to Liz Greene, sex was referred to as "the little death" by the Elizabethans, owing to its blissful final moment, the almighty orgasm. You know how some people (perhaps yourself) believe that the only way to get close to god is through the sexual union? This is connected to that notion. The little death can create a potential life, the ultimate nexus through which humans exit the cave of the womb and meet the world. The Saturn in Scorpio lesson links this death directly to debt. How, you ask? Back in the day before we were liberated, women were considered chattel. We were our husbands' possessions, legal prostitutes of a kind. And sex was the currency we trafficked in. Wives provided a service—sex leading to the production of progeny. Husbands entered into an economic contract with their wives through marriage, and so it went. There was little room for the notion of romantic love. This is how the Scorpio lessons came to be associated with other people's money, debt, and the like. Wives owed husbands sexual debts, and husbands owed wives financial ones. Often these debts became millstones that sunk marriages. This is how Scorpio, the sign of sex and death, came to be associated with debt—the debt of the marriage contract.

The Underworld

Even if you know little of astrology, you're likely familiar with the sultry, sexy, seamy sign of Scorpio. No matter what your sun sign, when you think Scorpio, you likely imagine a femme fatale standing in the corner with a cigarette and a flask planning her next revenge plot. Scorpio is ruled by the planet Pluto. Pluto was the god that abducted Persephone from her lovely life as a maiden in the fields and took her into the underworld, to Hades. This was the place where the dead roamed. Not exactly hell, but not exactly heaven, either. It was, to put it politely, a dark place. This is where Persephone was raped of her innocence and identification as Demeter's daughter. Before her initiation in the underworld, her name was Kore. When she reemerged she took the name Persephone, symbolizing her rebirth and transformation. With Saturn in Scorpio, women resist change because they know that they will be totally transformed by it and go through a series of rebirths. Anyone who has given birth will tell you that it hurts like a bitch. When Saturn lands here, he makes you feel change in every molecule of your body. You can't avoid its ramifications. That's probably why you do whatever it takes to avoid it. But all of this is the golden call of Saturn's lesson as he moves through Scorpio. Your pain can set you free, girlfriend, like no other pain can.

> ## ♏
> ## Famous People with Saturn in Scorpio/Eighth House
>
> **Goethe**
>
> **Martin Luther**
>
> **Elisabeth Kubler-Ross**
>
> **Marilyn Monroe**
>
> **Queen Elizabeth II**
>
> **Marlon Brando**
>
> **Sigmund Freud**

If you were born into this lesson, you are a woman who understands pain—probably oceans full of it. Women born into this lesson seem set up for pain, so much so that the time comes when they simply offer up their wrists for slashing, because why expect anything better? The various tortures start at a tender age for Saturn in Scorpio girls. Relationships can be devastatingly disappointing. Daddy may fail you before you can even build up an expectation for him to do anything better. Often this signature is found in the charts of those who have a lot of death in their lives. One woman told us stories of deaths that started at the age of seven (her first important Saturn transit). First a great-grandmother, then a young friend hit by a car, followed in quick succession by three other grandparents, an uncle, a great uncle, a litter of kittens (at this point she began to think she was cursed and responsible for the death around her), and finally the last grandparent when she was twenty-one, at her third major transit of Saturn. These were just the most important people she lost. All in all, by the time she entered her early twenties, she had been to twenty funerals. This is a number usually found only in war-torn countries where people grow sickeningly accustomed to the idea of burying their loved ones. But with Saturn here, this kind of living always at the edge of death can become almost routine. This was Saturn's way of telling her that death was as common as breath. It's not that the pain of separation is any less intense when Saturn makes its home in Scorpio. The pain is deeply felt, and even studied. The commonness with which death can present itself can create a forced detachment from the brutality of the trials of Saturn in Scorpio.

The other extreme is that those born into the Saturn in Scorpio lesson experience not a whit of literal death in their lives. Some don't attend funerals at all, so death is foreign, a mystery. Still, though, these women can carry an irrational fear about death, worrying excessively about it coming to claim their loved ones.

Death Defying

There can be a morbid paranoia around the idea of death when Saturn is in Scorpio. Even for those who don't experience death as literally as in the previous example, there is often a rich fantasy life around the

idea of death. Chances are that extremes like ice-climbing are out of
the question for you and your loved ones. Sometimes there are elaborate funeral fantasies and planning for the worst. The opposite extreme
is possible as well. The shadow side of the obsession with death is a
fearlessness so complete that jumping out of planes can become the
sport of choice. Sometimes people with this placement choose to flirt
with death, to tease it so that their (sometimes unconscious) fear can
be eviscerated. These are the braver types. Or maybe not. Maybe it's
all a ruse.

Sexual Healing

And what of sex? This is the place where women experiencing this
Saturn lesson can experience the heights of heaven or the depths of
hell. Saturn here, disturbingly, can be connected to childhood sexual
abuse and trauma. There grows a guilt associated with anything sexual that can be so consuming that it sometimes takes the crisis of the
SR to heal it. There is sometimes a strong internalization of the Catholic ethic that sex is dirty, sex is dangerous, sex can lead only to
destruction. This can be linked to direct experiences where sexual
acts are forced, or it can just be a feeling, an energy around the
child/young woman with this Saturn lesson embedded in her karmic
signature. Sometimes there is an unspoken knowledge that there are
sexual problems between the parents. Again, this can be just a feeling. Because Saturn is so representative of the father, often the daughter becomes a substitute for the father's thwarted advances toward the
mother, and his sexual advances are felt by her. Sometimes, rather than
sexual abuse, there is violent physical abuse from the father, or the
threat of this. Even when the abuse is physical or verbal, sexuality can
be an uncomfortable undertone. If you were fortunate enough to be
a Saturn in Scorpio woman who never had to endure such a legacy,
thank god for small favors. If you were to explore the secret closets
of your family history, however, you might find some things that make
you cringe.

Coming of Age

With Saturn in Scorpio, as you began to come of age, starting in puberty, sexual feelings may have been heavy and intense. Feelings of guilt and shame may have predominated. Sometimes this results in a promiscuous phase, an attempt to hide the fears that are swirling beneath the surface. In other cases the opposite occurs—Saturn in Scorpio girls can be the very latest bloomers of the zodiac when it comes to sex. Many wait a long time, for the "right person." There are extremes with this placement. We met women who had slept with half of Manhattan and others who refused to talk numbers. And then there were those death-defying Saturn in Scorpio chicks who betrayed the current cultural norms and had fewer than three partners. They never went through a "bad girl" casual sex or "experimental" phase, even in college. This is a form of self-preservation with Saturn in Scorpio, because deep in the soul these women feel that when they give away their bodies, they are giving ALL of themselves away.

This brings us to another element of this Saturn lesson. The dedication and zeal with which a sexual partnership is built can be an art form for Saturn in Scorpio women. They can be consummate architects of the sexual realm, just because they've spent so much time thinking and meditating about the meaning of sex. This is what sexperts sometimes call overcompensation. These femme fatales can talk and think about sex as if it were their job. It's a boon for their partners, who get the royal treatment, but in the end, the issues must be worked through so none of this behavior is unconscious. (If the issues are dealt with, the result can be a healthy, active, and deeply passionate sex life, the kind that a lot of people dream about.) The other extreme, again, is the frigid case. Sometimes the fear is so complete that sex is an anathema. They just avoid it. They don't get around to it, telling themselves that it's not that important, that they have other concerns. This is the domain of the Madonna/whore, by a landslide. Saturn in Scorpio women don't need the patriarchy to instill this duality in them, because it's built right into the DNA. Astrologer Linda Goodman gave us a famous teaching about Scorpio: "When she is good, she is oh, so good . . . but when she is bad, watch out!"

Father Issues with Saturn in Scorpio

Who was your father, really? Do you feel like you ever really knew him? If you did, if he was there, did you always feel as if he had a secret life? For women born into this Saturn lesson, fathers often remain a mystery, even if they are present all the time. The nature of Scorpio is subterfuge, and even if your dad tried to be transparent, you may have always had the feeling that he was hiding something. Often this feeling is linked to sexuality. Many women report affairs and dysfunctional sexual relationships between their parents that were revealed to them only at the SR. There is often very little physical affection in the household, teaching the young Saturn in Scorpio girl that touching is bad and dirty. Saturn here indicates that the father, even if he tried to do right and love right, somehow received a seedy projection from his daughter. Money and debt can be issues for the father as well as for the daughter. He may have felt guilty about not being able to provide for you properly. He may have been tightfisted, carried a lot of debt, and not allowed your mother to have any control over the money. Another possibility with Saturn in Scorpio is that your dad was totally absent from your life growing up, either due to death or some other circumstance. If he was present, there's a good chance he was emotionally cold and distant; in other words, he may have been dead to you, even if you lived in the same house.

On the other hand, your dad may have been able to provide you with healthy, transformational experiences. Maybe he guided you through difficult times and taught you how to make it on your own. He may have shown you that despite the fact that life is hard, with hard work, you can overcome any obstacle.

Facing the Saturn Return with Saturn in Scorpio

Saturn in Scorpio is well schooled in secrets. The crisis that occurs at the SR often requires a bloodletting, a letting go of the deepest and darkest truths possessed by the unconscious. A woman can hold shut the door to Hades for only so long. Arms eventually get tired, and at the SR, the forces will keep coming in their various forms to burn down the door until you let go willingly. Therapy is a beneficial addition to the war chest of any girl at the SR, but for women born into the Saturn in Scorpio lesson, it's almost a necessity. When the floodgates are finally opened, friends and family can do only so much to mop up the mess. The beautiful news is this: the deeper the wound you reveal, the deeper your healing will be. Saturn just asks you to shed the old skin and uncover the indestructible power that you have always truly possessed. This you can hold onto forever, dear one.

In the late twenties, all of these issues start to come to a head for those born into the Saturn in Scorpio lesson. Sexuality can become a raison d'être, for better or worse. Some people experience the feeling that their very life is somehow dependent on sex or lack thereof. Sometimes a partner can show up who completely alters the sexual landscape. There can be sexual obsession, deepened promiscuity, or enforced celibacy. We hate to tell this to those of you facing your Saturn Return in this sector, but during the SR your fate may be that you just ain't gettin' any. Despite your charm and beauty and sexual voraciousness, during your SR you may not be able to lead another to your willing bed despite fresh 250-thread-count sheets and all the right toys and tools. Another possibility is that sex at this time has dire consequences. If you have it against your better judgment, not relying on your intelligence and instincts, you could end up with a sexually transmitted disease, or worse. Unwanted pregnancy is also a possibility when you fail to have sex for the right reasons. We're not going to try and tell you what those right reasons are, because you know them in your heart. Suffice it to say that at this time of your life, it would behoove you to listen to your heart and your head rather than your nether regions.

From Transaction to Transformation

Other scenarios at the Saturn Return are connected to debt. Sometimes a long-standing debt comes of age during or prior to the SR. If you've ever borrowed money from a friend or relative, at this time you might find that paying them back is absolutely necessary to preserve the relationship, and vice versa. If you have your resources tied to another individual, such as a husband or business partner, you might find that money becomes a source of conflict. Sometimes sex and money merge here: you may find yourself using sex as a weapon of withholding or promising sex in return for compensation. Maybe your lover owes you money and you won't give it up until you're paid back. Or maybe your lover pulls this trick on you.

Death

Crises at the SR for this placement concern death in both literal and figurative forms. Because fear of change tends to chain those with Saturn in this sector of the chart, at the SR, change becomes inevitable, sometimes drastic. It can feel like an earthquake or a nuclear explosion. Remember, we are dealing with the energy of Pluto here, and plutonium did not get its name by accident. Because Scorpio is the sign of disintegration, the SR here can feel more drastic, more dramatic, more fraught with blaring sirens than for any other sign. Even if there is no literal death around you at this time, you may feel as if you are dying. (But that's why you're reading this book, so you don't have to go through that!) Your feelings about death, loss, and change are likely to be dredged up at this time, and the way you grapple with these highly charged emotional issues can give you the resources needed to smother neurosis in the months and years after the SR has ended. Reclaiming ownership of these issues, rather than letting Saturn whip you into submission with his ironfisted fear mongering, is the best way to self-medicate at the SR.

Real-World Saturn Return in Scorpio Stories

Kara: Feeling Like a Sexual Leper

Kara met her boyfriend Peter when she was twenty, just prior to a major transit of Saturn. He was her first lover, as she had waited patiently for the "right" guy to give her virginity to. As a child she'd suffered sexual abuse at the hand of a male baby-sitter, and this contributed to her fear of sexual intimacy and created a deep, deep need in her to trust anyone whom she would be naked with. But right away she got pregnant. When she talks about it now, in her early thirties, she can almost laugh at the absurdity of it all. "I couldn't believe that I could get pregnant the very first time I ever had sex. I thought it was impossible, but it seemed like it was just my luck." She had an abortion, didn't tell her parents, contracted an STD from her boyfriend (with whom she ended up staying for seven years, one complete Saturn cycle), and spent the next few years worrying about birth control and his infidelities. Ever the Saturn in Scorpio overachiever, she recalls performing oral sex on her boyfriend the very first night after her abortion. She didn't want him to suffer without sexual gratification even for one night, because she wouldn't be able to sleep with him for three whole weeks. Even at this sensitive time, she would do anything to please him, and the best way she knew how to please him was through sex. But the truth was, after the abortion and the STD, every experience left her feeling as if sex was something that she would inevitably be punished for. Incidentally, she recalls their sex life fondly. Even with the shocking start, their sexual relationship grew to be one of the best parts of their union. But still, she broke up with Peter the moment that Saturn entered the realm of Libra (seventh house; see Chapter 7, "The Other") and spent the next few years completely alone, barely even dating and healing from her breakup. This seemed an oddity to all her friends and coworkers, for Kara is beautiful, intelligent, funny, kind, and charming—a catch for sure. The moment that Saturn started its journey through the Scorpio sector of her chart and her SR began, she felt as if she was a man repellent. She briefly dated a few men but slept with none of them, and when she did fool around, she almost always ended up feeling used. She felt like she couldn't get laid to save her life. Halfway through her SR she started therapy and began to ferret out the bitter memories of her sexual abuse. The memories came flooding back and hence started her transformation. She began to connect the pain of this initial wound with the pain of all the wounds that she'd suffered since. This was the true healing. Toward the end of her SR, she met the man to whom she is now married. She continues to do the inner work, but the scars are less visible on her surfaces.

Julianne: Drowning in Debt

When Julianne came in for a reading at the start of her SR, she was feeling absolutely terrified. Several years before, she had started down the path of making one of her lifelong dreams come true: she had applied and was accepted to a prestigious graduate school, so she could immerse herself in English literature. This was all well and good but she didn't have any way to pay for it. Her parents, meager of income but generous of spirit, offered to act as guarantors for her loan, because she didn't qualify. They expected that when the loan came of age Julianne would be safely ensconced in a stable teaching career and that the loan would be paid back without delay. Julianne decided that teaching full time was not her destiny shortly after she graduated from her program. The problem was that her freelance gigs and part-time teaching job didn't meet the high monthly payments she had to make for her loan. She took economic hardship, unemployment deferment, and finally forbearance to stall the repayment of the loan. In her own mind, she would have been content to simply let it go and deal with the consequences of defaulting. But she couldn't, because her parents' credit rating, their mortgage, their very life depended on Julianne making timely payments. Eventually, after screaming arguments with both of her parents (mainly her father), she was forced to buckle down and take a full-time job, even though there was a Peter Pan inside of her that said she should be living as a starving artist. By the time her SR ended, she made enough money that she could cope with loan payments without worry. She took a certain pride in making payments, and by age thirty-two she made a solid dent in her principle. Her payments were lowered, and she was able to go back to freelancing and having the life she really wanted. Her contentious relationship with her parents has improved drastically, and she knows never to get tied up in such a debt again.

Beth: Facing Her Father's Demons

Beth's dad lived with her, but from a very early age, she remembers him as a vague, distant presence in the house. Even when he was sitting on the couch next to her, she felt like he was nothing more than vapor most of the time. But when she got out of line, even the slightest bit, he flew into a rage and made his presence known. As she aged, the violence grew worse and worse. She always felt as if he was secretly angry with her, as if he blamed her for everything that was wrong in his life. When she was fourteen, her father chased her up the stairs, and when she locked herself into her room for protection, he broke the door down. Anger was the only emotion he showed, and it was the only kind of attention he ever paid to his daughter. Beth couldn't wait to escape from her house, and she did so at the age of twenty. Whenever she returned, on weekends or holidays, she and her father would barely speak. He didn't speak to anyone, really. But at least the violence ended at this point because Beth had learned not to provoke him.

A year prior to her SR, Beth got a disturbing call from her mother. She told Beth that her dad had been to the doctor that day and got some alarming test results—he had prostate cancer and it was at an advanced stage. Beth felt sick to her stomach, but not because she was worried about her father. She had so long ago turned off her feelings for him that the nausea she felt was in response to noting that she didn't feel bad—that indeed, she felt nothing. When he went in for surgery a few weeks later, she had to visit. Her mother was a wreck, and Beth comforted her. When Beth went in to see her dad, he sat stone silent and pretended that it was because of the painkillers. But she knew his silence was the result of the emptiness of their relationship. He couldn't seek comfort from the daughter whom he'd alienated many years before, and he knew it. The experience felt cold and steely and stiff.

Survival Skills for Saturn in Scorpio

Experiment with Tantric arts.

Pay back your debts.

Try belly dancing.

Get a financial planner.

Read Elizabeth Kubler-Ross, Anne Sexton, and Sylvia Plath.

Practice Kundalini yoga.

Read the *Kama Sutra*.

Go to sex shops.

Attend a séance.

Watch *Six Feet Under*.

Consider psychoanalysis.

A few weeks later, she talked with her mother and decided to come clean about how awful it was for her to see her dad in the hospital—not because she was concerned for him, but because she did not feel any compassion. He was feeling better by this time, so she was less worried about laying the story on her mom. And suddenly the floodgates were opened. Her mother, having gone through harrowing weeks of fear about her ailing husband, cried and defended him. But Beth could not be stirred. Even after learning that her father had been abused as a child, she couldn't forgive him for what he'd done to her. But she did decide to start therapy at this time. A few months later the doctors found that there was still cancer remaining in his body and that he probably had only a few months to live. One night Beth's boyfriend raised his voice to her, and in a flash she was brought back to her childhood and began to sob. The next day she went to see her father in the hospital. And she sat there and told him everything. Everything she was angry for and, equally, everything she'd come to terms with. She told him that she loved him. It was true. The next day, he passed away. And Beth cried oceans for him, and for herself. Finally, a few months after her SR ended, her healing began in earnest. This was breakthrough season for her therapy. A few years beyond her SR now, Beth feels like a psychologically healthy woman, not a victim of abuse.

Saturn in Scorpio Potentials

These are just a few of the possible scenarios that can occur during the SR when Saturn returns to Scorpio. Issues with comingling assets, secret schemes, sexual depravities of various sorts, and drastic, painful change that rend your soul are other possibilities when you are involved in this Saturn lesson. It's heavy-duty stuff when Saturn visits you in this sector of your life. You will change, even if Saturn has to drag you by your hair into the boat and endure your screams of protest as he paddles you through the Styx to the other side. It's a trip worth taking, even if it sometimes feels like it's on the *Titanic*.

If your karmic contract had the Saturn in Scorpio signature on it when you were born, you are a deep and tender soul. By the time you turn thirty, you've probably gone through much healing, renewal, and upheaval. And you've likely resisted every single change as if your life depended on it. Your sacred rite is transformation. Every time you give up the resistance and meet Saturn on his terms, you win another round. Think about the changes that scare you the most and make them. Even if you feel like you are dying, you can be sure that you'll be reborn again.

Sagittarius

Sagittarius needs freedom. Sagittarius needs to fly. Sagittarius needs truth, undiluted and pure as snow. Sagittarius needs to go abroad. Sagittarius needs to know. Sagittarius needs to think, to muse, to expand her world. Sagittarius needs her ideals, her belief systems, her soapbox. Sagittarius needs to understand. Sagittarius needs to eat books like bread. Sagittarius needs fierce independence. Sagittarius needs to teach and sometimes preach. Sagittarius needs to fuel her fire, to philosophize, to take her mind ever higher.

Higher Mind

SAGITTARIUS

Keywords/Issues:	freedom, aspiration, exploration, faith, optimism, curiosity, expansion, joy, truth
Ruler:	Jupiter
Symbol:	The Centaur
Element:	Fire
Modality:	Mutable
Opposite:	Gemini
Archetype:	Temperance
Key Phrase:	I Understand
	Sagittarius rules the hips and thighs
	Sagittarius is associated with the ninth house

The truth will set you free, but first it will piss you off.

—MARIANNE WILLIAMSON

Sagittarius is the sign of freedom and the search for truth. It evokes the gypsy spirit and the quest for what is truly global—the wisdom that connects us across cultures and centuries. It is where you thirst for knowledge, but not necessarily information. (Gemini is more interested in fact finding.) With Sagittarius one finds inspiration, meaning, more questions, and philosophical musings. A trip through the Saturn in Sagittarius lesson will bring you to your own true wisdom, because you, darling, are the true teacher.

If you were born with Saturn in Sagittarius or Saturn in the ninth house, or if Saturn is about to visit you in this part of your chart, you might ask yourself the following questions:

- Do you find it hard to have faith?
- Do you suffer from the grass-is-greener complex?
- Are you looking for the perfect spiritual path?
- Do you sometimes feel like you believe in nothing?
- Are you ever overwhelmingly pragmatic or compulsively logical?
- Were you brought up with heavy morals and dogmatic ideas?
- Do you ever feel hopeless?
- Do you have trouble looking toward the future?
- Do people accuse you of being "holier than thou"?
- Do "spiritual" things make you uncomfortable?
- Are you, rather, always searching for the path to enlightenment, only to find that you have exhausted all your resources?
- Do you feel as if you have to have the last word when it comes to ethical/moral dilemmas?
- Have you ever had problems with the law?
- Do you have a private soapbox engraved with your initials?

It's important to note that Saturn and Jupiter (the ruler of Sagittarius) are traditionally known to be at odds with one another. To put it in simplest terms, Saturn brings restriction, and Jupiter brings expansion. But they are both concerned with the law and the notion of righteousness and justice. When these two heavy cosmic forces tango, get ready for some manic-depressive sessions. Saturn says contract, conserve, and be realistic within your limits. Jupiter says to hell with that, the sky is the limit: more, bigger, better, and beyond!

One of the gifts of this lesson is that Saturn tends to filter poorly thought-out arguments through his careful sieve, and thus prevents the possibility of ridicule in intellectual duels. You probably win, all the time, because you are a careful thinker and shoddy analysis will not pass your test. You likely scoff at those who can't manage their arguments as well as you can. You have mental discipline like no other. Are your friends anxious about sharing wacky ideas with you? You're not likely to quickly buy into the existence of UFOs, conspiracy theories, or occult imaginings. People who know you know that in order to convince you, they'll have to trot out a lengthy and properly footnoted treatise that documents all the whys and hows. If you can't see it in front of your eyes, you are not likely to believe that it exists. Proof is a raison d'être for you, dear.

Rhodes Scholar

It's not easy to live under the thumb of your own heavy-duty scholarly barometer all the time. It's not that you're close-minded, exactly; you just happened to be born with most of the answers, right? This doesn't stop you from consuming books and books of literature and sampling foreign films and communing with the best of the bohemian sages and wandering sadhus. Deep inside, you want to know it all. It's just that you probably don't believe anything you hear. You might be a big-time cynic, refuting claims before your idealistic buddy even finishes his sentence about who may have been responsible for the latest political scandal. You might be the type that shoots down arguments before they leave the gate. Sagittarius is the centaur—half man, half horse—galloping his way through life and rarely stopping to see what he just knocked over, spilled, dropped, tripped over, or left behind. If you were born into the Saturn in Sagittarius lesson, you probably find this kind of oversight repugnant. You can't abide stupidity because you just don't have time for it. There are too many horizons to broaden.

Ism Schism

OK. This is not the easiest thing for us to say to you. But you might have some bigoted tendencies, too. This is in pace with your feeling that most people aren't as smart as you, or as well read, or as worldly.

Sometimes those born into the Saturn in Sagittarius lesson harbor just a few racist, classist, or other "ism" ideologies. This tendency is often engendered in childhood, when you may have been exposed to prejudiced worldviews. There can be a lack of tolerance, an inability to plug into the richness of diversity that those from different backgrounds can offer you. You might feel a little afraid of foreigners. You are on the path to a universal consciousness and Saturn is testing you along the way. Sometimes he might do so by surrounding you with dogmatic religious and social viewpoints as a child, and they can't help but stick to some impressionable part of your brain. It might be your lot to overcome the narrow-minded viewpoints of your parents, or early schooling, or some other primary patterning. Your beliefs might be so internalized that you're not even in touch with them at all. But the Saturn in Sagittarius lesson will force you to look at them at some point.

The other possibility is that there was no structured belief system in your home when you were a child, and you've had to figure it all out for yourself. Maybe your parents were so progressive that they allowed you to choose your own religion. Maybe there was nary a mention of divinity at home, and you longed for a god that seemed invisible. Maybe you were a Jewish child who couldn't figure out why there was a Christmas tree in the living room every December. Maybe there was no mention of god in your home because your parents were brought up believing that he was too stern a judge, and they rebelled against all forms of religion and spirituality.

I'm a Believer

The Saturn in Sagittarius lesson is about faith more than anything else. You are learning how to have faith in yourself, something you have probably hungered for all your life. When you are constantly tested by a search for the meaning of life "out there," it takes the onus off of you to find your own direction, your own faith. This is why many Saturn in Sagittarius women find it so difficult to achieve a sense of inner faith. Instead of looking inside, they crane their necks and get lost in books and philosophical debates about the nature of the universe, while conveniently ignoring the universe within. You may be a constant theory tester, and this outlook can cause you to court disillusion wherever your travels take you. You have often decided ahead of time that the hypothesis you are positing will fail, and although you always remember to do the investigation, you might have already assumed that it's hopeless. Ever the thwarted centaur, you'll likely continue the quest, but you'll shake your head with disenchantment because it's just so hard for you to believe.

Very Superstitious

Do you secretly fear black cats and avoid walking underneath ladders? The Saturn in Sagittarius lesson can cause you to go the other way and pay blind homage to ritualistic rules and regulations. If you've bought into any doctrine of religion, you might be the type to repeat the mantra in the perfect format and sprinkle the appropriate variety of holy water while you pray, in exactly the way you were taught. Deep inside, as you do these rituals, you probably don't think they're actually working, but you do them anyway, just because. Maybe your lifelong fear of faith is masking a secret belief that god is always watching and judging you, so you better fall in line.

Law-Abiding Citizen

The Saturn in Sagittarius lesson is also concerned with the law. You might harbor a fear of getting caught by the authorities for even minor transgressions, so that jaywalking could give you a slight coronary. You could have been the kind of kid that refused to shoplift, even when your friends were stuffing lipstick into their bras. Another possi-

Famous People with Saturn in Sagittarius/ Ninth House

Grace Kelly

Maria Montessori

Marcel Proust

Oliver Stone

Richard Nixon

bility is that you took a chance on something that you were sure you absolutely wouldn't get caught for, and you got caught. Some Saturn in Sagittarius folks have trouble with the law, from getting sued to getting arrested. Watch those security cameras, mama.

Jet Lag

Yes, you long to see the world. But sometimes culture shock can be so daunting that it keeps you at home. You may not be a big fan of foreign foods, languages, and cities. Somehow they could feel restrictive to you. You might have negative experiences with foreigners—perhaps that last boyfriend from Brazil turned out to be a world-class asshole. There's a kind of provincialism with this placement that's not easily overcome. You could feel simultaneously attracted to and repulsed by those from foreign lands. You want to know the nature of their accents, the spices in their foods, but somehow you just can't trust them, because they don't know where YOU come from. The bottom line is that Saturn in Sagittarius engenders a need to understand and, even more so, a need to be understood. This is where the shadow relationship with people who come from far away becomes a problem for you. (See Chapter 7, "The Other," for a discussion of the shadow.) With Saturn blocking your natural instinct to dash around the world and sample every culture, you may feel a real fear of striking out on your own, traveling, and getting involved with those that come from far.

Higher Ed

The Saturn in Sagittarius lesson is also about getting an education. You may have harbored fantasies of doctorates and dissertations, but something or someone (most likely yourself) may have gotten in the way. Maybe you didn't live up to your potential in grade school and high school, even though you were always ridiculously smart, and didn't get into your college of choice. Maybe you couldn't afford to attend the university you were accepted into and had to forgo an Ivy League school for a state college. Maybe you went where you wanted to, but frittered it all away at parties instead of focusing on academics. Maybe you floated from school to school, searching for the perfect alma mater. Women born into the Saturn in Sagittarius lesson sometimes fail to complete school the first time around, ending up credits short of their diploma. They still know that they're the smartest of the lot, but they have trouble finishing their degree.

Do the Right Thing

This is the classic placement of ethics for ethics' sake. You may spend many hours deeply contemplating your moral moves, but because this is a lifelong issue for you, you may have developed some rote defense mechanisms to deter guilt. The difference between right and wrong is something that you seek to understand with full clarity, but in the meantime, you might find yourself abiding by society's codes because of fear of retribution. Even when it comes to relationships, you may focus on "doing the right thing" to protect yourself from guilt or anger, rather than being motivated purely by compassion or love. As long as you've covered your ass, you believe, all should be right with the world, despite whether you're doing what you believe or not. Not that you lack compassion, darling. You do have it—loads of it. But when it comes to proving yourself the righteous one, priorities are sometimes shifted.

Father Issues with Saturn in Sagittarius

Was your dad a master of dogma? Did he mire you in the letter of the law, with no room for nuance? Was he cold and bookish? Did he seem to roam the world without you, lost in his ideas? Was he a bit of a bigot? Did he close his study door and ruminate? Was he close-minded and argumentative? Did he criticize your ideas? Did he thwart your early urge to be creative and free?

The Saturn in Sagittarius lesson can create a courtroom dynamic between women and their fathers. He may have been judgmental and coarse and have run the house with an iron fist . . . or a heavy gavel, depending on the circumstance. There may have been harsh moral judgments foisted on you when you moved beyond the bounds of his carefully constructed code of ethics. You may have had to set up elaborate schemes to avoid his punishments. When you climbed out of the window to meet your boyfriend at midnight, you were probably very meticulous about making sure the lump in the bed looked like you—not because you were doing anything wrong, necessarily, but more because getting in trouble may have been terrifying. He may have made you feel guilty, preemptively, for things you didn't even think of doing, thus keeping you in line. And you probably didn't do those things you actually considered wrong. Because then there would really be guilt to pay, not just punishment.

On the other hand, Dad may have been smart as a whip and taught you a lot about life. He may have bred a deep hunger for knowledge in you, a curiosity that runs immeasurably deep. He may have been something of a sage and introduced you to various philosophies. Perhaps he valued higher education and encouraged you to pursue it. He could have been a very funny guy, splitting your side and hamming it up for you all the time.

Facing the Saturn Return with Saturn in Sagittarius

When you hit the SR, you may start to feel that your usual round of faith testing has increased to crisis level. You may have a genuine crisis of faith at this time, the kind that can change your life. If you've lived all your life in a dogmatic prison, you may suddenly break out into a new belief system. Perhaps you grew up rigidly Catholic. Suddenly, you may begin to feel that yoga is the right path for you. You may give up old rituals in exchange for new ones and make some dramatic changes. It might just seem suddenly that your old belief systems no longer support you. You may see all the creaks and cracks in the armor of an antiquated religious system, if you hadn't already begun to question them. You might, alternatively, begin to question the foundations of a philosophy that you've been living by. Maybe you've been a vegetarian since the age of fifteen, because you knew it was the right path. When you hit your SR, you could have a total transformation in your philosophical foundation that changes your attitude toward eating meat. Perhaps you'll read the literature of the local animal rights group and feel that their stances are hypocritical. Then it's off to McDonalds.

Don't Join the Moonies

Because you are apt to feel a bit of crisis now, as all of those experiencing their SR do, make sure that it doesn't drive you to the cultish edge. You are so hungry for meaning and purpose now that you might dispense with instinct and join the nearest group of true believers—believers in anything. You are seeking truth, and you could feel a bit desperate for it now. Make sure you keep your healthy sense of skepticism alive at the SR, because you'll likely need it.

Get Outta Dodge

An unfortunate reality of Saturn's passage through the Sagittarian sector (ninth house) of your chart is that you may experience problems with the law at this time. Any past indiscretions can come back to haunt you at the Saturn Return. Those traffic tickets you've been

Survival Skills for Saturn in Sagittarius

Get out of town—travel, travel, travel, and broaden your horizons!

Experiment with ethnic foods.

Learn a new language.

Immerse yourself in foreign cultures.

Ride horses.

Define your truth.

Study new religions and philosophies.

Go to bookstores and lectures.

Go back to school.

Be a teacher.

Meditate on the open sky.

Live free or die.

stuffing in the kitchen drawer may suddenly transform into a very nasty note from the courthouse that you have to attend to. You should be very careful right now when it comes to legal issues. Don't take any chances—be vigilant about not breaking the rules. You may not actually get sued, but you may have some anxiety about the possibility. You could simply find yourself thinking about any criminal intent you've harbored, even if you didn't go through with it.

Wise Woman

This is a time for becoming truly civilized through the wisdom you've collected throughout your life. It's time to decide on the role you will play in society, and you are likely ready for your real education. When Saturn returns to the Sagittarian sector of your chart, you may find yourself ready to go back to school, whatever that means for you. If your higher education was thwarted and you didn't follow a traditional path to a degree, you may find yourself ready to consolidate and do whatever it takes to get yourself enrolled in the right program. This is the time that the eternal search for truth bears fruit. You may have to do some grunt work to get there, but if you're willing to, the rewards are likely to be great. Cutting corners for a greater purpose is one of Saturn's favorite ways of showing you his path. If you have to take out loans, get a roommate, or work an extra job, it's apt to be worth it to you. In your next Saturn phase, you are going to take your knowledge into the world and get some recognition.

Travel Restrictions

Some people have problems getting anywhere during the SR in Sagittarius—that is, getting anywhere far away. Saturn can restrict you from engaging in long-distance travel during the SR, unless it's for an educational purpose. So if you want to study abroad or acquire a new business skill that takes you overseas, it shouldn't be a problem. If you're doing it merely for pleasure, Saturn might throw some obstacles in your way.

Save the World

Toward the end of your SR, you may find yourself thinking more than ever about social responsibility. That Habitat for Humanity website might start to look very, very compelling right about now. Go join the Big Sisters. Or sign a petition. You may find your inner activist during your SR. This is because you've finally come to really understand right from wrong. All the struggles around meaning can be clarified now. You now begin to know what your soul really needs.

Real-World Saturn in Sagittarius Stories

Tara: Losing Her Religion

Tara was always the smartest of all her friends. And she had pretty smart friends. But hers was a quiet intellect, and she didn't use it for academics. She hated the textbooks at school and preferred to read on her own, knowing that she could provide herself a better education than her teachers could. She read voraciously, eating up series after series of books. She went to lectures at the local bookstore, all by herself, even as a child. She was raised Catholic, and her parents were very serious about their religion—church every Sunday and shiny shoes a necessity in the pews. It seemed totally formal and emotionless to Tara, right from the start. She hated it. They forced her to go to Sunday school, too, something she disliked even more than church itself. She read the passages in the Bible herself and liked what Jesus had to say on the whole. But the fire and brimstone didn't sit well with her, and early on she grew sick of being threatened with purgatory for minor sins.

She rebelled, sampling various religions through text and experience. She went to synagogue with a Jewish friend and studied Buddhism and the yoga sutras. But none of it resonated with her, so she gave up by the time she entered college. She decided she was a Marxist and married herself to the concept of dialectical materialism. A consummate recovered Catholic, she shunned the idea of religion and spirituality and had little time for those that practiced such things. She changed majors five times and left school with a lot of credits but no degree.

When she was twenty-eight, she started to have an extreme crisis of faith. Her job was unfulfilling—a paper-shuffling, go-nowhere position—and her relationships were insubstantial. Suddenly she was possessed by the need to leave everything behind. She decided to quit her job, break up with her boyfriend, and start the process of selling her possessions, not knowing exactly where she would go. She'd lived in Seattle her whole life and had loved it, but at the SR she felt a powerful urge to part with everything she'd ever known. She decided on Paris. She began to study French and calculated that she'd have enough money to get there within six months' time. (At this point she was almost twenty-nine and halfway through her SR.) But numerous obstacles got in her way. Her father got sick, and she had to delay her trip. She was forced to stay in the apartment she'd intended to leave, living a bare-bones existence. She figured she'd get another temporary job to keep her afloat until she could leave, but there were none to be found, as the Internet bubble had just burst. Even jobs at coffee bars were sparse. So she lived on pennies and read books as she waited for her father's surgery.

During this time of difficulty and drought, she renewed her relationship with her father. She spent a lot of time at the hospital by his bedside. One day, he asked her to pray for him, and she smiled but scoffed at him secretly. She was convinced that prayer did nothing. When he went in for his surgery later that week, Tara was distraught and felt completely helpless. She was inspired to pray, purely because she couldn't think of anything else to do for him. And she knew it was what he wanted, so she decided to call out to some form of a higher power. She closed her eyes in the pallid waiting room and started to talk to God. To her great surprise, she felt connected. Suddenly, she felt an energy rising through her body, a divine presence. This energy didn't feel at all like the righteous brimstone-hurling entity that she'd known as a child. It felt like a comforting, protective light that made her feel sated. There was nothing threatening or strange about it. It was simple and profound, and she felt safe in its embrace.

Her father came through the surgery. Tara decided that she wanted to go back to school, to study theology, of all things! She was inspired by her experience at the hospital and began researching programs. As luck would have it, she found a program at a university in Paris, and she was off. She finished her degree and is now teaching, at age thirty-three, in the City of Lights.

Saturn in Sagittarius Potentials

This is just one possible scenario when the Saturn in Sagittarius lesson is met at the SR. You might experience problems around faith, spirituality, personal philosophy, the law, higher education, or ethics. If you were born into this lesson or if you're simply experiencing Saturn's passage through this sector of your chart right now, your higher mind is calling you to get serious about the journey to your highest truth and greatest faith. You are capable of becoming truly cultured and worldly. You could be known as something of a sage and a beacon of light for others. Saturn asks you to create a spiritual path or personal philosophy that makes your world broader and brighter. Once you possess the truth there is no need to impress it upon anyone. Your only responsibility is to live it. This is the highest teaching, and you are the highest of teachers.

Capricorn

Capricorn needs a mountain to climb. Capricorn needs milestones. Capricorn needs positive authority figures. Capricorn needs discipline. Capricorn needs structure. Capricorn needs to see the manifest and the real. Capricorn needs skepticism. Capricorn needs to crawl before she can walk. Capricorn needs quality and lasting value. Capricorn needs status. Capricorn needs tradition. Capricorn needs to build and build over time. Capricorn needs the timepiece. Capricorn needs responsibility. Capricorn needs calculation and timing. Capricorn needs ambition and conquest. Capricorn needs support. Capricorn needs nothing. Capricorn needs the world.

The World

CAPRICORN

Keywords/Issues:	ambition, discipline, high standards, conservativism, result-mindedness, structure, giving form, rules, limits, definition, authority, duty, reservedness
Ruler:	Saturn
Symbol:	The Goat
Element:	Earth
Modality:	Cardinal
Opposite:	Cancer
Archetype:	The World and the Devil
Key Phrase:	I Use
	Capricorn rules the skin, hair, teeth, and bones
	Capricorn is associated with the tenth house

Success achieved, he never stays/for only by never staying does he not depart.

—LAO TZU

When Saturn lands in the sign he rules at your birth, forget the SR, your whole life feels like one big final exam. This means serious business; don't lose your sense of humor. You will need it, because Saturn is going to test your reserves. Are you up for the lifetime of the champions? Truly there is no time for half-stepping around the responsibility of your life's great mission (and only you know that). By the devil, you will feel it in your bones. We mean this quite literally as this, more than any other placement, will enforce the Saturn call to duty right into your physical structure, so if you feel like rigor mortis is setting in, start climbing your mountain. This lifetime demands action, and you cannot tolerate just sitting by and waiting for something to happen. You know you have to march forward step by strategic step, Capricorn.

When Saturn is in Capricorn or the tenth house at birth, or he's approaching this sector of your chart as you read this, you may ask yourself the following questions:

- What mark would you like to leave on the world?
- What is the greatest fear that holds you back?
- What guilt is weighing you down?
- Has healthy skepticism turned into straight-on negativity?
- Do you have too many rules or too few rules?
- What are your priorities?
- How do you rule yourself?
- Do you use wisdom or a whip to get your life on track?
- What insecurities keep you on a plateau?
- What would the ideal father have been like?
- How do you provide structure and discipline for yourself?

Mount Rush More

Here your karma is about establishing yourself firmly in the world. You may have felt the pressure of this great climb since birth and either put yourself in accelerated programs or perhaps taken cover in one of Capricorn's drugs of choice, marijuana. The fear of success is great here. Don't panic just because your ruling god's name is Pan. Saturn is patient and in fact loves the one-step-at-a-time approach. Yet missed opportunity, inconsistency, and broken commitments really get his goat, and he'll sick one hell of a paralyzing guilt trip on you if you indulge in these activities.

Once you know what you must do, but then go and blow the opportunity, that is when he whips the guilt chains around your spine. Procrastination and time wasting are the two biggest ways to summon his mind demons in the form of self-recrimination. Saturn will do a number on you with guilt tripping when he visits his own sign. You may experience some serious depression sessions. The only way out is through concrete but constructive action within the right frame of time. This means foresight, planning, scheduling, consistency, and follow-through. You know those "coach" (not the handbags, honey) plans to get your life together? Capricorn loves all of those handy little time-management tools and getting into the power of the "now." Procedure, method, and efficiency are as pleasing as punch for Daddy Saturn when he's in Capricorn. He cannot get enough because he knows it is the way to get you to the top of your mountain. Let's be clear here. This climbing theme does not mean "over" others (Saturn wrote the book on ethics, after all), nor do we mean to suggest that Saturn wanting the world means unlimited credit at Saks Fifth Avenue. We simply suggest that whatever your karma is, you should fulfill your worldly obligation to the highest level. Even if your karma is of the highest spiritual, unworldly vibration, chances are Saturn will pull you out of your meditation cave and into the world to serve.

Who's the Boss?

There is no question that in career matters you need to call the shots, run the show, and rule the roost. Boss is a four-letter word with this Saturn. You are not keen on submitting to authority figures unless they have accomplished the impossible task of winning your respect. Even if they move mountains and walk on water, you will have your doubts and sticks to shake should they dare show you a human foible. On the one hand, you are looking for the perfect mentor, structure, strategy, and sage of worldly wisdom. And yet, your inner tyrant will meanly reject any outer help, especially if it smells of softness. This is the hard core of the hard-core dictator potentials. Unless Saturn has refined your power and ambition/drive/fear combination into wisdom, we pity the fools who get in your way.

Like Fine Wine

Working together, Saturn and Capricorn have a plan to get you into some high-level maturity, but as with all fine things, this comes only with the proper seasoning: time. This life will cook you with Saturn's wizardry of preparation, timing, and execution. We hope that by the time of the SR you have learned to have mercy on yourself and realize that your large-scale plans take time. As long as you have a draft and are consistently taking the steps, there is no reason to go three rounds with your superego. Speaking of superego, does your conscience ever let up on you? If by age ten you were not at the top of your chosen field, your inner agent may have unleashed furies of reprimand on you. We know one woman who never forgave herself for not having the lead in the school play during her senior year of high school. Forget that she was also class president, newspaper editor, and lead singer of a rock band; she could focus only on the thing she did not accomplish.

Fashionably Late

We don't mean you are late in terms of punctuality; you are probably right on the dot when it comes to showing up for others. Fashion-ably late refers to trusting that you can relax a bit and come into things in your own time even if it feels late by comparison to your social milieu. Remember the other Saturn dictum: quality over quantity. The standards here are at their highest. What will it take to assure you that you are getting better with time? If you are already on the fast track to success, it will only get better. You actually get younger, lighter, and funnier with age. The Saturn in Capricorn comedy duo of sarcastic retorts and one-liners are priceless. Saturn here, more than anywhere else, ensures that if you are a late bloomer, you will see that it was all worth the wait. But please know we aren't suggesting that you wait, as in sit and wait for something to finally happen to you. Keep plugging away, master your skills, do your work, keep your heart open, and wait to see well-earned results. This Saturn loves the hard-edged, hard-work, build, build, build approach to your career that you can tangibly feel you have earned. Man, oh man, woman, will this Saturn let you feel you deserve anything you don't sweat and bleed for? There are no shortcuts, but there is a bit of a turtle/hare potential here. Try not to get ahead of yourself and lose the race when your wiser inner animal knows that if you just plod along, you will reach the destination.

High Maintenance

Have we mentioned that your high standards could put a five-star hotel out of business? Seriously, whether you are a millionaire or a broke Betty, you demand quality with a capital Q. It doesn't even have to be flashy or glam the way a Leo or Pisces would have it, but it does have to feel expensive and lasting. Nothing insults you more than cheap quality or shoddy workmanship. You will not tolerate it in yourself, and hell hath no mercy on the sloppy Joe who tries to pass a cheap replica by you. You demand the real thing. If that sloppy Joe lives in you, don't do it. Don't sell yourself short on quality to save a buck for the more practical side of you, or the cheapness will start to eat away at you like bad calamari. Even if the status-loving part of you succumbs to

♑

Famous People with Saturn in Capricorn/ Tenth House

Princess Diana

Leonardo da Vinci

Emily Dickinson

Albert Einstein

Bob Fosse

Zsa Zsa Gabor

Audrey Hepburn

Adolf Hitler

the conservative side of Capricorn and you opt for the replica, you will feel it under your skin. The same way fake gold can turn your skin green, anything that is fake or compromises integrity in any form will turn a Saturn in Capricorn green. It's so not worth it. Don't even cheap out on the groceries; cut coupons if you have to, but get the good stuff or you'll end up spending just as much money on filling your Prozac prescription to cope.

Hard-Knock Life

If it's not difficult, you probably won't value it. But if it feels *too* difficult your resistance and fear to even try could downright depress you. You push yourself harder than anyone in the world, but sometimes you really feel you won't get started until the world forces you to make your move. Are you aware that you sometimes asked to get your ass kicked because you do the same thing to yourself? Ease off on this hard-drive approach before it brings you to your knees. Unclench your teeth, stop pulling out your hair, and just make up some new rules for yourself. Chances are you have too many or too few rules. And in the latter case you probably just abuse yourself silly for not having any rules. You need to know that there are real consequences to your actions or lack thereof to motivate you. If you resist the climb out of fear of failure or fear of success (actually just as common), you will suffer the consequence of inertia creeping in. The more you fail to take action, the more exhausted and stiff you are apt to feel. For you, the worst thing is knowing what you should do and then going back on it. Follow-through, consistency, and practice are the mandatory nuts and bolts to make your life work. We know you need facts to prove exactly how and why all of this works. The proof is in the way you feel. If you pride yourself on being a tough woman, chances are you've taken the rules a bit too far. On the other hand, if you are floating around with the weight of your unlived potential on your back, you probably gave up on yourself and bought into the fear fallacy. Thus, we offer you this pearl from Neale Donald Walsch's *Conversations with God*: "FEAR = False Evidence Appearing Real."

Father, Why Hast Thou Forsaken Me?

Before we really get into the kind of father you might expect with this lesson, let's first address an overarching potential of feeling: the inner authority you so need and were probably denied. Life might actually feel like a perpetual struggle to uncover your inner power, authority, and esteem to achieve good things and make your mark on the world. Either you experienced it being taken out from under you, or you were never cultivated or nurtured by either parent. There could be a longing for the inner father to finally lead you with care to the base of your mountain and at least give you some guidance, if not a map or a clue as to how to get where you are going.

Father Issues with Saturn in Capricorn

Was your father steady Freddy? So reliable and consistent you could set your watch by him? Either this man won the upstanding father of the year award for his morals, ethics, and integrity, or he was smoking pot down in the basement while cutting coupons. If this man did not accomplish great things or live up to his outstanding potential, you were sure to have had one depressed daddy on your hands. Maybe he was the tough-love type who felt he could really show you his love by acting like your football coach or manager. He probably imbued some kind of "tough as nails" approach to fathering. We hope it was a nice mix of love and discipline and not just the latter.

In extreme situations your childhood could have felt more like the military. Did your father make you rise early, make your bed, and drop and give him twenty just to see if you were on point?

Chances are this father was at the top of his profession, a master of something. He most likely had the command of the home, too. If he wasn't around in your childhood, you might have sought out other tough-love master teachers. In some way this father taught you that the good things in life take work, and the good people in life will make you work hard. The father may have put too much emphasis on the practical stuff—the work and achievement—so that you never felt loved beyond your grades and your gold stars. Somewhere along the line, this father may have wittingly or unwittingly imparted a twisted message that your worth is determined only by your status in this world. This can be positively back breaking before you even get started. If your father had a tyrannical and critical streak, watch that you have not internalized any reprimanding, self-fulfilling failure prophecies.

Similar to the Saturn in Cancer lesson, the Capricorn roots may indicate that any lack of loving fathering goes back to your father's father or beyond. Perhaps a rigid, cold, authoritarian great-grandfather started a bad cycle of dictator dads. In general with this Saturn, you find a grand issue of repression somewhere in the relationship with the father's side of the family. Either he was repressing some fear, self-doubt, guilt, or other monster and taking it out on you, or there was some other issue thrown into the rivers of denial. Denial is the key issue here. So long as everyone pretends the ugly stuff does not exist, shame and guilt will run the show. If your father did not confront these demons, you might have inherited some unfinished business in your own life. What are you denying, repressing, or hiding in shame? Denial can also mean the ways that your father took the cheap route and denied himself the good things for fear of not acting practically or conservatively.

On the bright side, if your father was in good shape, he may have embodied the wiser, gentler side of the Capricorn nature that just wanted to teach you step-by-step how to reach the peaks in life. On the positive end, he may have just taught you how to appreciate the finer things in life and go for the real thing, not the fake. Choose the quality every time, even if it costs a little more. We hope he taught you to love yourself every step of the climb and not just when you reach some illusory peak. If not, as you reach your SR, Saturn can stand in as the loving father to help you.

Facing the Saturn Return with Saturn in Capricorn

With this Saturn you can't help but care how the world sees you, and at the SR you could swear you are on candid camera. There is really a sense that the weight of the world is on your back. There is a pressure that the world will see every mistake you make and remind you of every failure or flaw. The fear of judgment is strong here. Is it too late? Did you blow it? Don't forget you are the biggest critic and you might have to quiet your negative jurors. Don't forget to consider the big picture and the whole mountain before you go to town with the self-recrimination trips.

Mastery

On the one hand, the world will project authority onto you and ask you to set the rules and standards. And on the other hand, you will feel as if you constantly have to prove your worth with real results. At the SR, you may feel it is time to own or move toward mastery of your field. Inwardly you know that you came here for nothing less than self-mastery. You know deep down that you deserve the status and the access to really show what you are made of. You just have to keep the faith. If you're not there yet, the show is not over until the fat lady sings. That fat lady is Saturn. A great teaching for coping with this SR: "What you see is not all there is." True Saturn screams: "Don't buy anything sight unseen." And yes, we know he will judge the book by the cover, as well as the content. He wants it all top-notch, no question. But when it comes to your evolution, don't forget that even gold was a work in progress. And honey, you are no base metal even if the alchemy is still in process.

No Free Lunches

At the SR, the urge to be with the upper echelon of your field will be of utmost priority. You have likely worked your tail off and expect the

Establishment to give you the props you deserve. You will pay your dues slowly and steadily as long as you feel your efforts are dignified and worth the cost. This Saturn more than all others is always thinking of consequences. If the outcome looks good and the struggle seems validated by the potential payoff, there are no mountains you would not climb to get there. The hard part is finding something you consider worthwhile to really sink your teeth into. If you haven't found it already, the SR is about finding the worthy challenge to tackle. You are so full of reserve, skepticism, and doubt that it takes a lot to convince you to start the long, hard ascension. Yours, more than any other Saturn, is of the "if it looks too good to be true, it probably is" school and the "there are no free lunches" school.

High End

At the SR, you want the world to see how high end you truly are. You want supreme status, the kind that will outlast Chanel, Ferragamo, and Prada put together. In fact, you would not mind your own name engraved on the world. Not that you would ever be so tacky as to admit something like this, but at the SR you are probably thinking bigger and better. Capricorn is reserved by nature and would just like to have the status recognized without a big fuss. You never want to lose your cool authoritarian demeanor. You could look as if you are organizing a corporate event when you are just buying your friends a drink at the bar. Capricorn gives you the natural A-list aura even when you're in your sweats. The blessing of this SR is that you have learned how to impress the world with your natural worldly ways. You look and feel expensive, because you are.

As the World Turns

At the SR, you might struggle with the feeling that the world is passing you by because your goals are so great and time is moving so quickly. Don't get ahead of yourself, darlin'; time is on your side. If you avoid that idle, noncommittal, fearful fretting that could offset your pace or throw you down into the depths of self-doubting despair, you will be on your way in no time. Chances are the real issue is that you don't even give yourself credit for the things you have tackled and conquered. With this Saturn, being hard on yourself is as daily an occurrence as the newspaper landing on the stoop with a thud. The inner tyrant is likely to remind you of the "would've, could've, and should've" at every crossroad. He just wants to push you a little as the climb gets steeper and assure you that the same dog won't bite you twice. Why not give up the regrets and cut yourself a little slack but keep climbing? If you haven't even figured out your path, Saturn could throw you down into deep despair. Or conversely, if you have bit off more than you can chew by moving up the ladder too quickly before getting the skills under your belt, Saturn will also have a little throw-down with your ego. If you block yourself with fretting and stewing over past failures, Saturn will try to drop-kick you back to the base of your mountain and demand you take the first step. Get on with your big plans before it really is too late. Drop the guilt baggage and the inferiority or superiority complex, and start scheduling the real discipline you want to master.

Real-World Saturn in Capricorn Stories

Felicia: Overachieving Overkill

Felicia, an only child, was a real father's daughter. Her mother had passed away when she was only a baby. She did everything to impress her hero dad to the point of wanting to be the son he never had. She was being set up to deny any of her own instincts and desires in favor of living up to his expectations that she would rise to greatness by age seven. This meant no girly time and nothing fun, frivolous, or without constructive purpose. She was taught to play to win from the start. If there was no purpose to something, it was a waste of her time. This was the overriding message from her father. It was all about the end result, making the grade, and getting the certificate—not about the process. There wasn't even room for trying your best. It was all about the results.

Felicia's father was the owner of a large real estate company in which he made a fortune, putting him in the role of provider supreme. Felicia had everything she needed except her father's time and warmth. He treated all of their encounters like a business meeting. He had a grand plan for her life by the time she was ten. She was put into all of the accelerated programs. By the time she was fourteen she spoke three languages, had traveled the world, and was being prepped for the Ivy League and to be the future president of the United States. The expectations were out of control, and this poor girl did not even have time to take a deep breath for fear she might miss an opportunity. She had no idea what she was even interested in. Instead, she had this overwhelming fear that if she wasted even a second in her life she would disappoint her father and lose his love and support. She lived with a secret terror every day that someone was going to find out that she really wasn't intelligent, advanced, or special enough to make it to the big leagues. Despite this fear, she pushed herself to the edge in hopes of defeating the insecurity and the vulnerability of self-doubt. She slept only five hours a night, never socialized, and studied like a fiend. She forced herself into every possible extracurricular activity available at her father's request. She had bitten all of her nails off and was starting to lose her hair at a young age from the amount of pressure she put on herself. The anxiety was also spiraling into a major depression during which Felicia stopped eating and sleeping. She felt like a machine with no feelings of her own. She had to keep trudging along on this brutal path that was laid out for her.

She was accepted at Harvard and started her preparation for law school as her father had ordained. There wasn't even a second thought or consideration as to whether she had any intrinsic interest in pursuing law as her career. It was just a rule that was set by her father, and she had blindly conformed to it. Her first year away at school was a major break for Felicia. What started out in the same vein of pushing herself to achieve soon began unraveling with her newfound freedom in the world beyond her father's. She'd never had a chance to rebel with the other teenagers. This was a foreign concept until someone passed her a joint at a party on campus. The release and the high she felt from just a few hits of the marijuana were enough to bring her house of cards down. She was hooked. Things took a major turn from this point. She ended up falling for a brilliant hippie boy and cutting all of her classes until she was finally kicked out of school. Her father was furious and told her he would never forgive her for such an embarrassing failure.

He cut her off emotionally and financially as well. She needed the liberation, as devastating as it was to be disowned by her father. She took the leap and started the long road of looking for the true dream she abandoned at age seven. What did she really want to do in this world? What was her real ambition in this life? These questions were too overwhelming for her at this stage in her life, so she just hid out with her boyfriend getting stoned every night. She needed the opposite extreme of underachieving just to get the pressure off her back.

At twenty-nine, she was living in Berkeley managing a bookshop around the time of her SR when she faced the real crisis of her life. Her two worlds collided. Her boyfriend of seven years dumped her for a high-powered lawyer in San Francisco. The wheel had come full circle. She woke up in a cold sweat realizing she still had no idea who she

Survival Skills for Saturn in Capricorn

Climb mountains.

Participate in any kind of boot camp or extremely disciplined program.

Stay away from marijuana or other drugs.

Break your goals down into manageable chunks.

Write a mission statement for your life.

Undergo deep-tissue massage.

Stop beating yourself up.

Become financially independent.

Follow a well-defined weekly schedule.

Create priority lists.

Create five- and ten-year plans.

Explore your relationship with your father and authority figures.

was. The inner terror of failing to do something great in this world was still haunting her. After years of pot smoking and slacking off, the inner tyrant had gained more momentum to torment her with thoughts of her abandoned potential, past failures, and feelings of shame. She knew it wasn't about going back to law school to please her father or impress her ex-boyfriend. She had to figure out what her true greatness was. A friend of hers told her of a group that was meeting to work with different self-help tools for artists, such as the seven principles of Da Vinci's success. This was very appealing to her. She desperately craved structure and guidance in her current despair. The process of working with the teachings and the principles and making them her own was a powerful breakthrough. It was the first time in her life that she was choosing the rules and creating the structures by which to live. She knew it was the beginning of a long, hard climb up the real mountain to first find out what she really came here to do. She was no longer trying to climb her father's mountain, or the most impressive mountain, but she was at the base of a path she chose for herself. No one could take this away from her. At thirty-one, she answers only to herself.

Saturn in Capricorn Potentials

Yours is a potential lifetime of the highest achievement in the eyes of the world. You actually can find yourself sitting right on top of it. Yes, it's a long and arduous climb, but every step in the ascension is worth millions to your personal growth. In fact, you have the potential to cultivate character of the highest integrity. You were born to do great things of the highest caliber and to leave an indelible mark on this planet. You have the potential for mastery in whatever domain you choose. If you can conquer fear and guilt in the process, your lifetime is truly a prescription for success.

You are learning to accept that yours is a life that truly gets better with time. Some may call you a late bloomer, but your ascent is of the highest caliber. You have the potential to realize that every moment in your life holds an opportunity to cultivate wisdom. You are a sage of sorts, the true wise woman who can tap into the highest quality of time-tested knowledge. Your journey may be ridden with tests about things that have real and lasting value versus things that rust over time. You have the insight and experience to know the difference. Because you sometimes feel older and sometimes younger than your years, you may possess a terrific sense of humor. People around you feel they are in the presence of a great teacher—one who has really been around the block. You speak from a rock-solid foundation instead of offering empty platitudes.

Aquarius

Aquarius needs to skyrocket into the future. Aquarius needs co-operation and the right cause. Aquarius needs to think carefully about the things that give her pause. Aquarius needs electricity. Aquarius needs to be independent, altruistic, and progressive. Aquarius needs the group, the community at large. Aquarius needs her goals, her wishes, and her dreams. Aquarius needs to tinker with things. Aquarius needs to drop the science and to use her mind. Aquarius needs to serve the public, to work for the good of the group, and to be kind to all. Aquarius needs her friends. Aquarius needs stimulation from all sources. Aquarius needs to freak out. Aquarius needs multiplicity, change, and new vibrations. Aquarius needs to shock. Aquarius needs to re-design and revolutionize.

CHAPTER 11

Community

AQUARIUS

Keywords/Issues:	equality, eccentricity, friendship, intellect, brother-/sisterhood, humanitarianism, unpredictability, altruism, independence, inventiveness
Ruler:	Uranus
Symbol:	The Water Bearer
Element:	Air
Modality:	Fixed
Opposite:	Leo
Archetype:	The Star, the Fool
Key Phrase:	I Know
	Aquarius rules circulation, the ankles, and the electrical system of the body
	Aquarius is associated with the eleventh house

To be "normal" is the ideal aim for the unsuccessful.

—CARL JUNG

Aquarius is the sign that says: "And now for something completely different," in the best Monty Python parlance. It embraces the strange, bizarre, weird, and wonderful parts of us. It is connected to group activities and collective humanity—the great unwashed. Aquarian energies can be detached, though, coolly offering analysis rather than empathy when it comes to close personal relationships as opposed to wider humanitarian concerns. When Saturn comes to visit this sphere, it can cause one to distrust anything unfamiliar or strange.

If you were born with Saturn in Aquarius or Saturn in the eleventh house, or if Saturn is about to visit you in this slice of your chart, you might ask yourself the following questions:

- Are you overly concerned with social acceptance?
- Do you feel like a lone wolf?
- Or are you too much of a social butterfly?
- What does friendship really mean to you?
- Does dispassion block your enjoyment?
- Do you feel pressure to bring the future into the now?
- Do you feel way ahead of your time?
- Do you alienate yourself, feeling like a freak, genius, or mad scientist?
- What shape are your friendships currently in?
- Are you working on your life's goals?
- Do people accuse you of being cold sometimes?
- Were you ever picked last for the team during gym class or rejected by cliques in school?
- Are you claustrophobic in crowds?
- Do you sometimes feel desperate to fit in?

Freaks and Geeks

If you were born into the Saturn in Aquarius lesson, you may have suffered a severe form of the kind of wounding many of us are familiar with to a certain degree—the popular-kids complex. But with you, emotions around this issue could be far deeper than you let on. You may have been ostracized for being "different" when you were younger. Whatever teasing you experienced may have been harder on you than it was on your peers. With this Saturn lesson, peers become the arbiters of everything. The attempt to fit in may have been a seminal experience for you. There is often constant anxiety around fitting in to social groups. If you achieved some degree of popularity in high school, it probably didn't come easy, even if you made it look effortless. If you were indeed the popular girl, you may have agonized about what it meant to be the desired one. "Is it all a superficial game?" you may have wondered. If you were on the other side of the window, looking in as a freak or a geek, you may have defensively hated the popular kids because of your incisive insight into their vapid existences. Liz Greene says of Saturn in Aquarius: "His own ideals, wishes, and his dreams are worthless when compared to the final and inexorable word of the great They."

So Lonely

The Saturn in Aquarius lesson can create a woman who knows what it means to be alone. You may be the type who feels totally alone even though you're surrounded by others. Or maybe you're the type who keeps only a few close friendships, because you know in your heart that quality supercedes quantity. You may shun new friendships for this reason. Whatever the case, loneliness could haunt you. You may feel so different and misunderstood at a core level that you won't let anyone truly know you. You might be the type to stand in the corner at parties, coolly analyzing your surroundings instead of engaging socially. You may have a superiority complex to make up for the deep chasm of loneliness that you carry with you like a heavy stone. You may partly embrace your inner freak as a defense against being ostracized. If you actively set yourself apart from the crowd with a freaky/geeky vibe, it would be difficult for the cool kids to chastise you, right?

Social Butterfly

The other alternative, a shadow reaction to the previous scenario, is the social butterfly syndrome, wherein you pack your PalmPilot so full of engagements that you haven't a moment to consider whom you're spending time with. You may not realize that you lack quality friendships in this case, because you're too busy bopping around town meeting with mere acquaintances. You might fill your life, and any void you feel inside, with parties and dinner dates and air kissing. As long as someone wants to pencil you in, all is right with the world. There can be a fear of being alone with yourself with this placement. If the eternal "They" aren't courting you the way you want them to, you are likely to internalize their criticism and decide that you're better off rubbing shoulders with a group of some sort. If you think they've got some glitter goin' on, perhaps some of it will rub off on you.

Famous People with Saturn in Aquarius/ Eleventh House

William Blake

Tori Amos

Carl Jung

Yoko Ono

Robin Williams

Joan of Arc

Square Peg

Another possibility is that you were so painfully shy starting in childhood that you are gripped by fear in social situations and find it difficult to relate. This can also keep you locked in loneliness. You could feel like a complete outsider. Even if you overcame shyness as you grew up, it could pose problems for you as an adult. You may still have a strong tendency toward introversion. People might perceive you as cold and compassionless, when in reality you are just analytical. You might tend to compensate for shyness by using logic to understand human feelings; for example, in order to avoid looking at your own painful perceived inadequacies, perhaps you spend time putting others under the microscope. Others also might see you as the cool cucumber that never gets out of control in an argument. People in your life could get frustrated by your ability to reason with them when they are enraged, because not a lot of things get to you—at least on the surface. It's not that you're devoid of emotions, it's just that they may be a bit buried.

Friend in Need

Often those born into this lesson suffer grave disappointments through their friendships and feel much bitterness because of this. Friendships can prove to be ridden with trials. There are sometimes betrayals and disillusionments that can cause you to end friendships, even after a long time. If you experience this even once, it can cause you to fear the very idea of intimate relationships. The people who seem easier to know, those who are kind and compassionate, very well might be the ones you avoid. You can sniff out the sort who will encourage you to reveal your true self, and your inclination might be to blow them off before things get intimate. Saturn in Aquarius often feels extremely vulnerable in friendship and will put up armor to protect herself. Maybe you keep telephone conversations and meetings brief so that your companions never have a chance to get to your core. You may have been stung once, long ago, and because your karma is tender in this area, you aren't likely to make yourself vulnerable with friends.

Social Stratosphere

You may also be accused of using others to get ahead in business or personal matters. You might find the glitterati wherever you go. There is a tendency toward social climbing for Saturn in Aquarius. If you admire people for their intellect, their talent, or their projects, you could try to insinuate yourself in their life, just to feed off the rosy glow of their energy and absorb their power. At some point, when they fail to impress you, you may just move on to the next influential man or woman in your midst. But in the meantime, your aim could be to advance your own position. Karma may call you on this behavior by causing others to try and do this exact type of thing to you at some point. Someone might use you for your contacts or your influence. Some far-flung acquaintance could cling to your own coattails.

People Are Strange When You're a Stranger

With this lesson, there can also be a fear of the strange and different. Saturn prefers the status quo, and when he bucks up against the eccentric energy of Aquarius, he could run into a fear of the weird. Are you hypercritical of those who don't fit your preferred mold? Do you default to the conservative side when it comes to friends? You may have to work through a disdain for those different from you. It could be healing for you to spend time with those from unfamiliar walks of life. Eccentricity might make you uncomfortable, but that just means it's a good idea for you to experiment with it. Despite any initial misgivings about strange folk, you might find that the weird ones always end up in your camp. If all your friends were gathered in a room, some of them might be accused of being freaks (but in a good way, of course). You might also collect friends who are older than you. Do you have friends who are seven years older than you, at least? This is Saturn's favorite number.

She's So Unusual

Speaking of weirdness, you may have a strong dollop of the strange within you. Perhaps you did not cultivate this on purpose, as mentioned earlier, as a way of setting yourself apart from the crowd and defending against anticipated teasing. Instead, you may have been born with a freaky streak of your own, and you may have no choice but to embrace it. You may not even realize it, but there could be something that stands out about you, something that people notice. It's just that you could be afraid of it. No need for this, sister dear. This is surely the very thing that makes people like you. We say raise your freak flag high.

Rebel, Rebel

Part of you is apt to want to stay in line, and the other part is likely to want to break out and start a revolution. With Aquarian energies stifled by Saturnian ones, there is often a repressed urge to rebel. Because you're probably willing to do just about whatever it takes to fit in and make people like you, you may not be willing to stir up the dust. But you could have a hidden hunger to change things, to create democracy wherever you go. When you witness poorly treated masses, you can't help but feel moved to help in some way. You are probably more inclined to extend your helpful hand to a stranger than to someone you know well. You may have above-average organizational abilities, and you can put them to work to make social change in the world. Democracy could be an important ideal for you. If you are involved in a group that is somehow undemocratic, you may make it your mission to change things, as long as you'll still retain your popularity in the end. This could be a lifelong issue for you, but you might take serious note of it when your SR hits.

Group Dynamics

When it comes to group activities, you may be a little reluctant and not much of a "joiner." This might be due to an early negative experience with group stuff. Were you forced to join things when you were a child? You may not be into the whole workshop thing, and perhaps you feel alienated whenever you have to perform within a group. If there isn't a sense of democracy in the group, you may automatically cast yourself (or be cast) as an outsider. Your group associations may also screw you over, somehow. You may even have claustrophobia, so that out in public spaces, surrounded by a group of people, you feel locked in. You might experience this again and again throughout your life.

When You Wish Upon a Star

Aquarius is also the sign of hopes and wishes. Your ideals come into focus when Saturn meets Aquarius. You might often feel like your wishes just don't come true. You may not bother anymore to blow eyelashes off your fingertips or break wishbones because you just don't believe that this kind of thing is in the cards for you. Rather than hoping for the outcome you want, you will probably have better success if you plant your wishes in fertile ground and tend to them responsibly. Proper feeding and watering of hopes and dreams is key.

The Saturn in Aquarius lesson offers you the chance to understand the real meaning of the word *goal*. It's not an easily discernable word, and although you could spend much time questing to realize your goals, watching them shift and reorganize and reinvent themselves every other day, you are blessed by your relationship to Saturn. That's because you are the sort that will be able to understand and realize your goals, for real, eventually. You could spend your lifetime searching for the right goals, the ones that perfectly match your soul. You may have a lot of goals, too many for one woman to handle on her own. Or maybe you're extra practical and don't believe that you deserve to nurse any truly lofty goals. You might sense that you'll never achieve them, so why set yourself up for a fall? The truth is that you are gifted with a rare ability to realize seemingly out-of-reach goals, so you should at least believe in yourself enough to try. Saturn wants you to realize that your goals are your meat and potatoes, so he may force you to reckon with them harder than other folks have to. In the end, when you get there, the struggles will have been well worth it.

She Blinded Me with Science

Just to give you credit, we want you to know, even if you have not yet realized your talent, that you are probably a born scientist. Your fine mind is gifted with the faculty of serious intuition, and you can ferret out details like a squirrel on speed. You are likely endowed with superior mental ambition, and you can probably visualize things that others can't. Even if you were never into dissecting frogs, you might find that you have a refined interest in all things scientific. Perhaps astrology turns you on.

Father Issues with Saturn in Aquarius

Was your dad ultraconservative and unforgiving when it came to eccentricities? Did he frown on the taking of risks and the exploration of new ideas? Did he seem to fear the future? Did he try to get you to stick to the status quo? Was he rigid? Was he cold and analytical? Did he have few friends and mostly keep to himself? Or did he fall into the opposite camp, socializing too much with those he didn't care about? Did he accuse you of being overly rebellious? Was he career-minded and serious, to a fault?

Was he weird in his own way, but neglected to recognize his own strangeness? Did he have some odd habits and foibles that you found embarrassing? Fathers of Saturn in Aquarius women can engender a fear of otherness in their daughters. They could be a little skittish and distrustful of people who don't come from their very own town or of those who look different, sound different, and think different. They might be overly cold and logical when it comes to the emotional realm.

On the other hand, your dad may have been amazingly quirky and cool. He could have had electric insights into life and how it works. Perhaps he was a big-time humanitarian, giving to this group and that group. He may have been a leader in social groups, chartering trips and organizing church outings. Was he a tinkerer? Could he take apart and fix your car like the best mechanic in town, without consulting the manual? He may have had some weird friends, but he embraced them warmly and taught you a thing or two about being nice to the less fortunate.

Facing the Saturn Return with Saturn in Aquarius

When you experience the first rumblings of your SR, repressed emotions about feeling like an outsider may start to come up. You may be profoundly aware of every moment when you feel less than accepted. Someone could ostracize you, and this could negatively affect your social standing somehow. You might start to reassess your friendships. If they're not serving you, you may decide to dispense with them. If you know too many people and have suffered from the social butterfly syndrome, you may now recognize that you have no real connection to the ladies you lunch with. So you might decide to trade them in for something more real. It's likely that it will take a crisis to make you face these demons. You may not be in charge of ending unhealthy friendships; instead, that may be up to the universe. So it could feel as if your lifestyle or your friends are taken from you, and you might feel once again left alone. But this time your solitude can serve you well. By the end of your SR, you're likely to know what kind of person you want to have in your life, by your side, and on your arm. You might experience retribution from those that have put up with your less-than-perfect attention to their friendship in the past few years. Someone who has allowed you to get away with not calling, not showing up, and general laziness around friendship could suddenly put his or her foot down and call you on your tendencies. But loyal and enduring friendships are the likely result of your SR, when it comes through the Saturn in Aquarius conduit.

Come on Down

If you make the choice yourself to disentangle from social relationships that aren't feeding you, you aren't likely to experience a painful fall from grace. But if you cling to empty relationships because you continue to believe that they will bring you influence, you could end up dealing with some unfortunate social circumstances. You may be suddenly shunned by someone whom you've admired. You may have to ungracefully exit from a group situation because of an embarrassing circumstance. Someone that you believed honestly liked you for you could turn out to have been using you for his or her own social-climbing activities.

Get into the Groovy

If your life experience has been less than experimental, you may now feel the urge to break out and try new things that you've been too afraid of in the past. Maybe there's something you've secretly longed to try out, but you felt that the people in your life would be critical of it. Maybe you want to experiment with new social roles and lifestyles. An external event can occur at the SR to bring you into closer touch with whatever your inner needs are. You might find yourself in unfamiliar territory, and you may feel a little bit afraid. But if you embrace this type of fear at your SR, it is likely to be a force for deep healing in your life. This is the best time in your life to take chances and try new things. It's OK to be a rebel now. If you've been involved with a group of some sort that you've felt suffocated by, now is the time when you will feel the need to leave. This could be painful, but it is also likely to be liberating. It might just spur you on to further explorations of the experimental variety.

Got Goals?

More than for any other Saturn lesson, Saturn in Aquarius brings your goals into sharp focus. Aquarius rules your goals, wishes, and dreams. At the SR you might suddenly feel as if you are standing on the precipice, disoriented and without a goal in sight. You may have always had trouble with long-range planning and wanted to do a million things in your starry-eyed future, but perhaps you could never quite wrap your brain around the one that made the most sense. At the SR, you could find that you *really* have no idea what you want to be when you grow up. But, holy falling house, Dorothy, you *are* grown up! You might start scrambling wildly for a goal to fit the lofty nature of your mind and begin to worry that nothing could possibly be good enough.

If you're working a dead-end job, this is the time when you are most apt to start rethinking that five-year plan. Do you want to pursue graduate school, a move to a new city, or a new artistic endeavor? With Saturn in Aquarius, the SR initiates a time of somewhat desperate goal seeking.

Real-World Saturn Return in Aquarius Stories

Melissa: Friendship 101

When Melissa was a young girl, she always felt like an outcast. When she was just seven, her family moved to a new town in the middle of the school year. She had to enroll in the second grade late, entering a classroom full of kids who had known each other since nursery school. It was a small community, and Melissa recalls feeling totally outcast, right from the start. By the time she met her peers, they were already a close-knit group and were reluctant to let her into the fold.

She played catch-up for years, doing whatever she could to fit in. First it was having the right lunchbox. She came to school with a Barbie box but soon found that Josie and the Pussy Cats were de rigueur at her school. By the time she acquired her first pair of Sergio Vallente jeans, Jordache were the rage. And so it went. She felt like she was always one step behind. She was picked last for teams in gym class and consistently had the feeling that people were talking about her behind her back. She especially had this feeling when she stood almost within earshot of a group of people. She made a few good friends, ones that she kept throughout her life, but even into high school, she longed desperately to be popular, to fit in with the other kids at school.

When Melissa entered college she was absolutely ready for a change. She could start fresh and make a lot of friends and not have to worry about her baggage any longer. No one would know about who she was before. She joined a sorority and made it the focus of her life. She had a group of friends now that would be there for her no matter what, an official sisterhood. She organized a ton of social events, and she was always on the go. Rarely did she spend an evening at home with nothing to do. But she never made any deep connections to any of the girls in her sorority. Her relationships always felt a little superficial. She always had someone to study with, to grab a coffee with, and to go to parties with, but she still didn't have anyone whom she could really talk to.

After college she remained active in her sorority and moved to New York City along with a bunch of the girls from her house. They all lived in the same neighborhood and dated the same group of guys, from a fraternity at their college. The group didn't disperse even after they graduated. Soon Melissa was working full time at an ad agency and socializing after work every day. Happy hour, brunch on the weekends, movies a few times a week—her date book was always filled. And she thought she loved it. She would review her week on Sunday nights, and if there was any day without a social event, she'd make a call to fill it. This went on for years, until she hit her SR. When she was twenty-eight, she suffered a fall from social grace. One of the girls she'd gone to college with had always had it out for her. They had a falling out, and in response she started to spread rumors about Melissa. The rumors stuck. Suddenly Melissa found herself shunned by the group and unable to fill up her calendar. People whom she'd been drink-

Survival Skills for Saturn in Aquarius

Evaluate your friendships.

Join Greenpeace or PETA or the local antiwar group.

Buy vintage clothes—the stranger, the better.

Read science journals. (Or watch the Discovery channel.)

Spend quality time with friends.

Socialize with those who make you a little bit uncomfortable.

Take risks.

Be a revolutionary.

Pursue your goals—all of them.

Let your inner freak out of the closet.

Shake things up.

Be socially experimental.

Start an "Everything I'll Do Before I Die" journal.

ing and dining with for years wouldn't return her phone calls. She was devastated. All the old feelings came back. She felt like an outsider again and didn't know what to do with her time. She turned to her old friends from high school. The problem was that they were already disgruntled with her because back in college she had virtually disappeared from their lives because of her involvement with the sorority. So Melissa found herself approaching thirty and virtually friendless.

After some months in therapy, she realized that she'd been filling her life with the noise of empty socializing simply to cover the wounds of her childhood. Fitting in was all she longed for, and now, with no group to marry herself to, she felt totally alone and was forced to face her demons. She saw for the first time that she'd put aside her most important goals in favor of socializing. Rather than focus on creating an independent life for herself, over the past seven years she'd been socializing as if it was her job. She took the opportunity to really look at her career, and she began to reevaluate her direction with a zeal she'd never felt before. She had a great epiphany—she saw for the first time that she had a tremendous amount to give. She'd spent so many years trying to plug up the vast void of nonacceptance she felt around her that she never had a real opportunity to think about the mark she wanted to make on the world. Toward the end of her SR, she started volunteering with an outreach group for teen girls in crisis. It changed her life completely, and soon she left advertising to work for the organization full time. Slowly and carefully, she started to rebuild her relationships with her old friends, and she began to make new ones. But she invited into her life only those whom she really wanted to be close to. She decided that she wouldn't make plans with anyone whom she wouldn't want to have over to her house for a long, intimate dinner. Melissa's rule of thumb worked, and she made it her business to have only quality friendships. Now that her SR is over, she loves spending time with the few important people in her life. She keeps busy but makes time for quiet, contemplative time with good friends. And her work has become the central focus of her life. The moment she decided to make changing the world a substantive part of her, everything in her life began to transform.

Saturn in Aquarius Potentials

This is just one possible scenario when Saturn lands in Aquarius. Other issues could come up around your goals, wishes, hopes, and dreams. You might feel alienated, ostracized, and cast out. You might also encounter problems with any group situations you've been involved with.

But there are many benefits here as well. You could learn to be the most open-minded and progressive chick in town. You can embrace your uniqueness, and even flaunt it. You can love everyone equally, with little favoritism. (This could lead you to become a true humanitarian.) It might be very healing for you to work in groups toward positive social change: volunteering could really change your life. You can shake up convention and bend the rules. You can have flashes of intuition that are fairly mind-blowing. You can achieve your goals. You might end up a true hall of famer. And, best of all, you can learn the true meaning of friendship. Embracing your inner freak is one of the best ways for you to create your own, necessary revolution. Go forth and be freaky, sister. This is the way that you can change the world.

Pisces

Pisces needs to drown in divine nectar. Pisces needs the fantasy, the vision, and the dream. Pisces needs surrender. Pisces needs the land of the gods. Pisces needs to dance. Pisces needs the music, the mysticism, and the mermaids. Pisces needs to try on different roles. Pisces needs to merge, melt, and mutate. Pisces needs synchronicity and the numinous. Pisces needs to rescue and be rescued. Pisces needs her compassion and her complexes. Pisces needs to relinquish victimization. Pisces needs pampering and poetry. Pisces needs sanctuary and solitude. Pisces needs baths, swimming pools, and oceans. Pisces needs drinks and spirits. Pisces needs the gateway to resurrection.

CHAPTER 12

The Source

PISCES

Keywords/Issues:	the sacred, illusion, delusion, obscurity, empathy, surrender, escape, fantasy, projection, dreams, phobias, imagination, an open channel, merging, dissolution, the invisible, redemption, forgiveness, compassion, poetry, mysticism, music, miracles
Ruler:	Neptune
Symbol:	The Fish
Element:	Water
Modality:	Mutable
Opposite:	Virgo
Archetype:	The Hanged Man and the Moon
Key Phrase:	I believe
	Pisces rules the lymphatic system and the feet
	Pisces is associated with the twelfth house

Life is a beautiful opera, except that it hurts.

—JOSEPH CAMPBELL

195

Pisces is linked with fantasy, mysticism, and the spiritual world. It often seeks escape from the mundane, trivial, or grosser elements in search of a place better than it can find with Xanax or a day spa. Pisces seeks a place where there is no more laundry, loneliness, or lying. Have you always had the feeling that there must be more to life than this? Has your life been a search for the sublime and the transcendent? Do you wonder if you have a "savior in session" stamp on your forehead as the ten thousandth victim begs you for rescue? Are you dying to merge with something greater to get out of yourself? Do you often struggle with crazy, lonely feelings? Pisces is the deepest of wells of the vast imagination and all of the archetypal energies that create your reality, and so when your life test is to enter this oceanic domain, get ready for the deepest waters of the unknown.

(Note: we make many references to Joseph Campbell in this chapter, as he opened up the transcendent Piscean world with his work on archetypes, mythology, and psychology.)

If you were born with Saturn in Pisces or the twelfth house, or if he is there right now, the following questions are worth contemplating:

- What are your escape mechanisms? Are they healthy?
- What is your relationship with the collective unconscious?
- How does music figure into your work and your life?
- How do you handle chaos?
- What inner demons show up in your dreams, phobias, and moments of paranoia?
- How are you confronted by all of your successes and failures?
- What do you bless, redeem, or overcome?
- How do you relate to the symbolic?
- How do you deal with the transition between the old cycle and the new?
- How have you incorporated significant threshold experiences?
- Do you use your imagination, or does it use you?
- Where have you fallen into the victim complex?
- Do you take the role of the rescuer/redeemer to avoid saving yourself?
- How do you seek transcendence?

- Do you struggle with any addictive tendencies?
- What is your spiritual purpose?
- What do you seek to merge with?

When Saturn meets the sign of the fish, your life task is to harness the vast ocean of bliss and chaos. Your universe could seem like a landscape of Rorschach drawings or an endless picture show that you would love to end. As soon as you feel you have reached the finale of one experience, you are thrown back into the birth canal for the next. Redemption, resurrection, and rebirth are exaggerated when Saturn has opted to teach you about the holy trinity of creation, preservation, and destruction.

Of course, we all go through the three stages, but with this Saturn placement, your life is centered and focused around how well you deal with each of the phases. Attachment to any part of the revolving cycle can lead to chaos and loss. As with all Saturn work, you feel like Sisyphus pushing the big rock up the mountain, only to watch it tumble back down. Thus, with Pisces, one of the major lessons is absolute surrender to the process, and this means the beginning, the middle, and the end.

Body and Soul

Pisces likes to trance right out of the body to the netherworlds. But strict Saturn could get fed up with the refusal to be in the body and throw you into some kind of physical boot camp to anchor your watery, ethereal ways. This lesson teaches that staying present in your physical form is a must. Even if it means dancing from here to Brazil, Saturn will challenge you to find the illumination you seek on the earth plane—right here, right now, and not elsewhere. If you space out, leave your body, and go into fantasy land for too long, you are sure to feel his weight bearing down on you in the form of depression, drainage, doom and gloom, or persecution fantasies. Pisces also loves to sleep its way out of all the pain absorbed from the suffering in the physical realm. Retreat is no problem for Saturn so long as it is constructive. Yet the real issues have to be worked out in present time, in the flesh, in a totally conscious way, regardless of all the behind-the-scenes dreamy unconscious prep work. If the evolutionary lessons are not channeled down into the bones and lived out in present time, be sure Saturn will drag you back to earth to work it out one step at a time. We already know Saturn is that part of us that will not let us skip steps, and when he joins with Pisces, he wants you deeply immersed, enmeshed, and surrendered to every moment of the process without looking ahead or behind.

Purple Haze

The vague, the mysterious, the unseen, and the vast oceanic experiences that cannot be put into words are also at play with Saturn in Pisces. Here we encounter the kind of inner experience that transcends the mundane, the verbal, and the ordinary. The kind of numinousness that can be expressed only through music, dance, poetry, and other subtle forms that speak directly to the soul. If that's too out there, you may just need to hide out in movie theaters to escape the harsh light of reality. When life becomes a quest for the transcendent, it is important to resist the temptation to turn poetry into prose. As Saturn is more comfortable in the known and concrete forms, it may be difficult to honor sacred yet elusive experiences—the kind of visions and dreams that are better left alone in their mystery. The minute you try to bring such spiritual dimensions down to earth, the pearl is lost and you might wind up sounding like someone who needs to be institutionalized. This is a sneaky, complex Saturn that does not conform well to words. Just like Pisces, this lesson tries to squirm its way out of being pinned down. In other words, here we are dealing with subtle experience, like a fine mist that will evaporate if you try to lock it down. This is the same way that poetry and music in subtle forms are better experienced than put into words. Did you ever hear a fish talk? Pisces are the spiritual fish within us that swim around in the murky mysteries of the unconscious. The same way that dreams seem to be speaking an alien language, you may feel as if you need a descrambling apparatus just to get through the day. No other Saturn placement makes you feel as if you live in the world of dreams and symbols. Confusion may very well be your middle name. But there is a way out of the illusion and delusion land that is Pisces: giving form to your fantasies, making your vision real, and solidifying the vague or nebulous potentials within you. Better yet, just turn off your television and get out of bed. (Pisces loves to hide out in beds and bathtubs.) Saturn wants you to live less in fantasy, where nothing gets accomplished, and more in reality, where your dreams can come true.

The Eternal Present

What is this elusive idea of the eternal present? Pisces is that part of us eternally searching for the happily ever after where there are no more dishes, details, or people to save. It is also the search for the perfect eternal resting place: the paradise imagined beyond time, space, and boundaries. Ah, the way it all sloshes together so nicely after a few glasses of wine. Saturn wants you in your body in present time to do your work, although you can still commune with things beyond. Because of your quest for the sublime, and acute sensitivity to the pain in the world, there is the danger of imbibing pills, alcohol, or any other promised land out of pain and suffering. Joseph Campbell reminds us: "The horror is just the foreground to a Wonder behind it." That wonder is not something that is outside of us in the form of a fairy-tale ending. Nor is it a heaven waiting for us only after physical death. It is about penetrating the mystery in this moment. The pain is in the temporality of time—in the losses, sacrifices, and inevitable endings that are so tied with this Saturn in Pisces. Time, being Saturn's domain, teaches the initiate to merge deeply into the heart of the mys-

Famous People with Saturn in Pisces/ Twelfth House

Bjork

Courtney Love

Kurt Cobain

Edgar Cayce

Walt Whitman

Woody Allen

tery of every loss, sacrifice, and ending to discover who one truly is beyond the roles she plays in her own personal ever-changing opera.

Facing the Demons and the Nightmares

One way to discover who you are beyond the role in your movie script is to explore the images of the unconscious by paying attention to your dreams. In some cases, Saturn in Pisces can block or censor the ability to recall dreams. In other cases, Saturn forces you to face your inner demons by staring them in the face in the unconscious realms during sleep. Any fears, phobias, or repressed traumas of the psyche will attempt to come to the light by working themselves out in dream scenarios. By working with the images consciously, you can begin to assimilate these outcast parts of the psyche. When these darker, repressed elements remain unconscious, you will be forced to live them out in the outer world via projection. In other words, you will project the disowned parts of yourself by attracting the right "hooks," or people who would be perfectly typecast as one of your own inner cast of characters. Don't underestimate the power of the unconscious. Even a crazy neighbor or a neurotic waitress you encounter is a part of your psyche screaming for your attention. Better to go within and see what this part of yourself needs in order to stop harassing you in the outer world. This is not an easy pill to swallow, as it means totally surrendering the victim roles and taking full responsibility for every aspect of your reality.

Tunnel Vision

When Saturn is in Pisces, the SR will throw you down into the depths of your psyche as if you are being thrown into involuntary psychoanalysis at every turn. It is as if life has been one series of birth canals after another. Saturn is working on your ability to smoothly cross the threshold between the known aspects of yourself and the unexplored depths with ease. There is absolutely no skimming the surface with this Saturn. He will throw you into the ocean and tell you to sink or swim. Navigating the depths of your inner world is no easy task, but the rewards are as limitless as your well is deep. As Pisces is also linked with the collective unconscious, when Saturn lands here it is challenging not to get enmeshed in collective images (fashion and music are filled with them) and feel you are to the point of losing your own sense of self. On the positive end, you can tap into the current vibe of the collective and act as a channel or an artistic medium to bring the new images to form. But you must also resist the pitfall of sinking down and identifying too closely with what you encounter in the collective psyche. In other words, rather than submerging yourself in "group contagion," Saturn will ask you to stay grounded in your self. The boundaries between the inner reality and outer influence need to be solid and firm to avoid such Piscean pitfalls as paranoia, deceit, and disillusionment.

Scrambled Self

To really know who you are on the deepest level, you must analyze the images present in your own psyche by looking into the dreams, art, or other spontaneous images arising from your unconscious. Jung taught that dreams are magnified manifestations in image form of energies in the body in conflict with each other. And Marion Woodman succinctly describes dreams as "photographs of the psyche as taken from the perspective of the unconscious." We have to decipher the language of our dreams to see what the unconscious is really trying to tell us. Again, with Saturn here, introspective work such as dream analysis is the lifeline. It may feel overwhelming and scary to enter into the abyss of the unknown and lose control. Saturn is all about sacrificing the safety of control, letting go of the known shore, and entering fully into the greater mystery of who you really are. It is about rejoining with the waters from where all life comes. OK, this may come off as some crazy, esoteric gobbledygook, but chances are if this is your lesson, your soul is translating and decoding these messages to at least let it all out on an unconscious level. This is the beauty of this combination: a lot of your Saturn work can be done lying down, either on the analyst's couch, in bed, on the astral plane, or in corpse pose at the end of yoga practice (a perfect Piscean pose).

Savior and Rescue Complex

Pisces is one of the most compassionate and empathetic signs in the zodiac and thus often feels sucked in, drained, or overwhelmed by the amount of need that she encounters from others. How often is the role of savior projected onto the woman with this placement, and how often does she feel compelled to respond? Of course, teaching the wounded would-be victims who land on your doorstep how to fish and help themselves will take you both a lot further in this healing process.

The deeper underlying lesson of Saturn has to do with saving oneself, of course. How do you come to the rescue of your own vulnerable, sensitive, and lonely feelings? How do you soothe and forgive the parts of your soul that have felt victimized? With this placement there could also be an interesting fascination with the whole Christ savior/redemption theme. In fact, the Christ consciousness, especially the teachings of forgiveness and loving thy brother, is the high-point potential with this Saturn. Ultimately the Pisces within us wants to merge back into the oneness and be saved from all feelings of alienation and splitting that create projection, separateness, and needless drama.

All the Universe Is Divine

Saturn in Pisces will pull one veil of illusion after another and yet still ask you to stick around and play the game to the end. He may strip the glamour from your mystical meetings with a bottle of wine by throwing you into a rehab, your savior/lover could be sleeping with someone behind your back, or your transcendental meditation guru could take off with your life savings. Wherever your vision was fogged out, Saturn will pull out the glass cleaner. Forget the smoke and mirrors; try it and Saturn will really set your house on fire. Nothing personal, just business ma'am. Saturn teaches us that delusion is a choice rather than a sentence, and it's painful only if we stand guarded with our denials and defenses. Yet, if we can see beyond the illusions and the temporary picture shows without either checking out or falling for the unreal, we can keep one foot firmly planted in this world with our souls plugged into our real source of otherworldly sustenance. The world is Saturn's domain, and thus you must live in it and appreciate it fully while you take care of your duty. In other words, pay your bills, do your dishes, and feed the dog before you take off for Fantasy Island.

Stop This Ride: I Want Off!

Pisces is the least worldly and most "otherworldly" of all of the signs and thus gives you the opportunity to be fully *in* the world but not *of* it. Joseph Campbell reminds us through his vast study of mythology and the Piscean realm of the archetypes, that if one can remain identified with eternity while participating in the confines of time, one will discover that the dimension of the here and now is the function of life. The next problem with the Piscean influence is in resisting the temptation to withdraw from the world when it is horrible. The horror, Campbell reminds us, is in fact the foreground of a wonder. The idea is to participate in the horror and the wonder and accept the first Buddhist principle: that life is suffering simply due to the temporality of things.

Disappearing Act

This brings us to another issue of Pisces: endings. Here we are dealing with the kinds of endings that vanish into the ethers—the mysteries of loss in general. With this placement you are sure to have wondered again and again how people including you seem to vanish into thin air. Whatever happened to so and so or such and such? Strange the way they just disappeared. What about your own infamous disappearing acts? With Pisces, it is not uncommon to experience feeling invisible whether you choose to or not. Of course, when you're in the mood to go incognito, this is a fabulous Saturn placement. But if you want your presence known, you may have to exaggerate your physical form, pinch yourself, or speak loudly so you know you did not retreat into your etheric double or back to the astral plane when you weren't paying attention.

Again, with Pisces we enter into the realm of the invisible and the unknown. With the painful unknown and unforeseen, if we can remain awake and unafraid we can recognize that it is all a great display of the eternal presence in the world. Here we learn more than ever that heaven and hell are simply the gods within us. All of the worlds we experience out there are merely projections from within us. The kingdom of heaven is within, and we can in fact ascend to heaven only from this inward place. Of course, this may seem like blasphemy if one gets stuck on the metaphor. The same way that poetry takes us beyond thought and into the mystery of who we are, metaphors are symbolic of something beyond the confines of literal denotative thought. It is when we get hung up on the metaphor that we risk fanaticism or a strong split between the concrete and the transcendent within us. The indefinable things could surely feel like nonstop neuroses unless you can find your own symbolic language. If you can paint it, dance it, or put it into poetry or music, you are on your way to psychic liberation.

Sacrifice and the Sacred

In the Saturn in Pisces lesson, sacrifice can take many forms. Your life's sacrifice can range from having to care for someone close to you who has become ill to sacrificing worldly concerns or just sacrificing the world you have always known in a quest for something greater. To make the heroic quest for the sacred, it is not necessary that you head straight for the Himalayas. Rather, just find at least an hour a day when you drop the worldly load and identification with your roles, stop the E-mails, turn off the cell phones, and explore the inner worlds and your vast imagination in search of who you really are. This is the true creative incubation: go back into the nothingness until new life can spring forth, which means emptying you out totally. It is all a means to get back in touch with what Campbell calls the "Thou" feeling of life, or the sacred divinity in every living thing in the universe.

Father Issues with Saturn in Pisces

When Saturn is in Pisces, the father may have felt invisible, as if existing in another realm altogether. This could be a result of alcoholism, other addictions, divorce, a time-consuming music career, or any other elements that could sweep him away from having a strong presence in your life. It may be that he actually lived in the house and yet seemed invisible or completely mysterious. As with the Saturn in Scorpio, this father may have had or seemed to hold many secrets or skeletons in the closet.

Another common father issue with this Saturn is feeling like he talked about you as if you were not even in the room. If he did not seem invisible, he may have made you feel as if you were. He may have further given you the impression that it was a no-no to explore your fears. The minute you wished to share your vulnerabilities, sensitivities, or fears, he may have slammed down the door of communication or just reminded you of how emotionally strong you were to reinforce his own defense of repression. There is the classic "what you can't see won't hurt you" syndrome with this kind of fathering.

On the other hand, this Saturn father may have been extremely sensitive, artistic, or mystical. He may have been a great filmmaker, musician, or closet poet. Maybe he was a combination of all gentle and mystical elements. Just as the fishes swim in different directions, the father may have had an elusive but cosmic quality, depending on which way the tide was rolling. He may have served as a spiritual teacher or seemed beyond this world. Perhaps as a child you wished he was less of a pushover or wished he was less influenced by the moods and mannerisms of people around him. He might have soaked up the atmosphere like a sponge. Was he the shoulder all the family would cry on? Or was he always hiding out as the victim? Or was he the slightly out-of-focus, "fuzzy" father? He may not have been too good with boundaries, but he also had boundless compassion for those who suffer in the world. Did you wish he wasn't so impressionable? Could he easily be impressed by a great film, work of art, or song? Did he bring music into your family? Chances are he was either a musician or appreciated music to no end.

On the higher side, this placement could indicate a father who really got the subtleties of life, understood the spiritual essence and oneness, and truly taught you the power of forgiveness. And maybe in some ways he seemed like the savior/Christ-like figure in your life. Whether he embodied this or not, the SR is about uncovering this wealth of forgiveness and spiritual essence within your own being.

Facing the Saturn Return with Saturn in Pisces

It might feel like an insensitive blaming of the victim, but it is a deeper spiritual teaching that puts the potential for the free will and conscious awakening back in your hands if you will also accept the responsibility that comes with it. Saturn begs you to rein in all of the projected blame and victim stances you have allowed to spill out over the years. If you refuse, he will just patiently hang out with you in isolation and fantasy until at the SR he decides enough is enough and pulls back all of the veils of illusion and self-deceit that you have been hiding behind. All the avoidant tactics and escape mechanisms will also be confiscated or exposed at the time of the SR. This reminds us of a time when our beloved Saturn teacher, Mata Amritanandamayi, decided that it was time to break a bad pattern with her ashram residents relying on their alarm clocks and fighting over the snooze function. This did not seem to guarantee they would be up in time for their spiritual practices anyway. Her message was that if we truly want to wake up and face the day we do not need an external alarm clock, because our inner teacher should wake us up at the time we are to get up. This is the perfect example with Pisces. Think of Saturn being the teacher that now has to rattle you awake from the inside to face the day instead of relying on external Saturn to force you awake against your will. At the SR, Saturn is taking away the external backups to see how strong the inner alarm is.

Phobias also result from projected or unconscious aspects of the psyche. For example, if you have an unconscious or unexpressed anger, you could experience it as a generalized feeling that someone is out to get you or that you will wind up at the mercy of someone else's anger. Pisces often suffer from claustrophobia, a fear of being confined or trapped in a space such as an elevator, a plane, or even a car in which they are not the navigator. Some psychological theorists believe this phobia comes from a fear of not having control. Mystics might claim it is due to a past-life experience of suffering imprisonment, being institutionalized, or being trapped or locked up in a confining space. Whatever the cause, with this SR it is likely that a central issue is in confronting all of the ways you have avoided your unconscious fears of confinement. At the SR, voluntary solitary confinement in a sacred space might be in order to get to the root of your fear of involuntary solitary confinement. Some ladies with their SR in Pisces have to confront the fear of involuntary joint confinement. That is for those who have come to love their silent alone time and fear that a relationship could challenge this. The struggle is probably a vacillation between your need for solitude and your need for merging. Saturn's solution will be to have you merge into the limitless potential of your highest self. By taking yourself beyond the boundaries of what you know through powerful art, mysticism, films, meditation, or deep psychoanalytic work, you can tap into the vast potential and know that you are part of something greater. This is the moment we've all been waiting for—Saturn's solution.

Real-World Saturn Return in Pisces Stories

Darcy: Emergence Through Emergency

Darcy was always an introverted and supersensitive child. Her parents divorced when she was seven, and she and her older sister ended up living with her mother in a small Midwestern town. Instead of making friends or hanging out with other children, Darcy preferred to commune with nature and the animals in the woods by herself. As she grew into adolescence, Darcy became more and more of a dreamy and shy artist who often felt invisible in her life. She spent most of her time hidden away from the world, creating until the wee hours of the night in her art studio. This was her sanctuary where she especially loved to work when the rest of the world was sleeping. She had very few close friends, as she felt most contented retreating from the stress and strain she encountered in social interaction. She felt most herself when she was alone in her own private sanctuary with her animals. She created beautiful mythic works of art that reflected the depths of her unconscious. The symbolic and abstract images that emerged on the canvas were comforting and healing for her. Yet the isolation started to creep in. By the time of her SR she felt so removed from the world that she wondered if she was even alive. She did not know how to bridge the gap. Every time she stepped out into the world she would come home feeling as if she had just been run over by a truck. This was all a result of her porous and impressionable sensitivity. She could not help but absorb the negativity and pain she felt around her. She would avoid it all and remain in her own inner sanctuary if she could. She did the minimum amount to sell her artwork to pay for her simple lifestyle. One small trip to the bank would require her to soak the negativity off in a long, hot bath or hit a bottle of wine. The wine started to become a necessity for coping with anything she would rather avoid, which she was discovering tended to be most things. She began to notice that the invisibility she felt had a lot to do with her own need to retreat and figuratively leave her body when she was in an uncomfortable position. She would do this with alcohol, going into her fantasy world or swimming right out of the present into another time and place as her body went through the motions of earthly matters. She did not see the point in having to live out a human incarnation. It felt like a lot of needless alienation, pain, and suffering to Darcy. The older she got, the more isolated and depressed she started to feel. She went through the worldly life on autopilot, dying to retreat back into her studio where she could finally come back into her body. There she could paint, dance, meditate, drink her red wine, and check out from her painful reality. Yet the profound sense of isolation and hangovers from the wine were fast catching up with her.

At the SR, Darcy felt as though she had been sucked down into the abyss of her psyche. She was struggling to distinguish between reality and fantasy. She was not even comforted by her artwork. Her dreams were fraught with nightmares of being confined, locked up, and abandoned. The loneliness was suffocating her from every corner of her soul. She knew she was losing it. The drinking was getting worse. Darcy stopped bathing, eating, or returning any phone calls. She stopped paying her bills, brushing her teeth, or doing anything else that kept her connected to reality. She was drowning. One night in the dead of winter, it all became too much for her. After consuming a tremendous amount of alcohol she found herself in the bathtub with a razor blade as she started to cut away at the soles of her feet with the intention of leaving marks all the way up to her wrists. She was only half conscious, but she decided that no one would even notice if she disappeared for real this time. It was early in the morning, and by the grace of a miracle, her landlord decided to bust through her apartment door in frustration over her evasion of several eviction notices. There he found her—just in the nick of time—and called 911. She was saved.

She spent the last year of her SR getting treatment for her addiction to alcohol and all of the emotional counterparts to her isolation and depression. In her treatment program, she discovered how

Survival Skills for Saturn in Pisces

Keep a pad of paper next to your bed, and write down your dreams or anything that comes to you immediately after waking.

Take soothing baths, or spend time near the ocean.

Listen to your favorite music.

Dance.

Sing or chant.

Paint, write poetry, or immerse yourself in sublime art.

Avoid drinking and drugs.

Get reflexology or lymphatic massage.

Create a spiritual sanctuary.

Turn off your phone when you need solitude.

Take vows of silence when you need to retreat into yourself.

much she loved to dance and how this could replace her need to check out with alcohol. She could stay in her body and yet go beyond it at the same time. This was the bridge she had always been looking for. The community at her treatment program also helped her with her fear of social interaction. It was the first time Darcy did not feel invisible. She was also discovering boundaries so that everyone else's pain did not have to instantly drain her and merge into her own reality. The most profound realization that occurred through this experience was her need to be part of something greater than herself while maintaining a physical presence on the earth. For her, the SR was about finally entering into her reality fully present.

Saturn in Pisces Potentials

Saturn endows you with access to an imagination as vast as the ocean. More than any other Saturn placement, this one gives you the grand assignment of bringing the collective vision to some kind of form. Whether you are a photographer, filmmaker, musician, or mystic, you have the sublime talent of plugging into the collective needs of the time and bringing the images into existence. You ultimately have the ability to see through all of the illusions of life. The things that are fleeting, changing, and temporal will not ensnare your soul when you tap into your own vast well. In fact, with compassion and sensitivity as your strengths, you have the ability to soothe and comfort many people still drowning in illusion. You may in fact be the lighthouse to save others who are drowning in escapist behaviors such as drugs and alcohol. But first and foremost, save yourself!

Conclusion

WHY WE NEED SATURN NOW

*Lord Saturn sits in front of each of us at every moment,
inviting us to surrender moment by moment to Reality that we
may be free.*

—SVOBODA

Moment to moment, getting ourselves fully committed to the right here, right now: that's why we need Saturn now. Not after the next television show, cocktail, or paycheck, but right now. Ask yourself this question: What would you want to be doing right now if this were your last right now? We don't have all the time in the world, because the world is running out of time.

The World

Saturn is the archetype of the world. Mythologically, he is symbolic of Armageddon, the end of the world as *we* know it. This is not a one-time shot we're talking about. Psychological Armageddon needs to happen continuously while we're still on earth. "Die before you die," say the Sufi mystics. He is the last dance. He's the last call, bright lights in your drunken face, get back to reality, last chance. Leo Buscaglia, a man who could pack a stadium to talk about love in the "me, me, me" 1980s, ended one of his famous talks called the Politics of Love with this statement: "Live every day as if it was your last, because one day you will be right."

In the past several decades, many of us have become air bodies or airheads, disconnected from the rhythms of nature, the cosmos, and the symbols of our inner world. As individuals and as a collective, we are constantly attempting to jet off the ground without being absolutely sound in our physical vehicle. And if we continue to do so, we will keep exploding, crashing, and burning back to earth. Do you have time to even connect to the ground beneath your feet when it takes hours to erase junk E-mail, pick up land lines and mobile lines, play video games, send instant messages, download files, and all the other digital anarchy of your life? How much more can we rush, abbreviate, generalize, and take the personal contact out of our daily lives? How many of your friends bother to type their full name in E-mail salutations any more? We are becoming one-initial human beings, the alphabet family if you will. Home visits seem archaic. Why bother when you can chat on-line? Handwritten anything lately? That's sooo Stone Age. Soon, a real phone call could feel like a major invasion, with the option of a three-initialed text message at your disposal. We have taken the E-ticket straight out of our bodies and straight to the world of the Jetsons. Earthly responsibilities? Can't we just PalmPilot our way out of those too? (Of course by the time this book comes out, PalmPilots might be as archaic as the Franklin Planner.) We could safely argue for the advantage of going back to the grounded extremes of the Flintstones at this point, by driving the cars of our lives with our own two feet.

Power of Love or Love of Power?

What's it going to be? This is the difference between a matriarchal approach and a patriarchal approach. The feminine, yin part of our souls, regardless of gender, invites us back into our bodies so that we can love the mother, the mater, or the matter within and without. Earth is the Great Mother, and she is dying a slow death at the hands of the presiding patriarchal will to power. When corporate profits supercede the needs of the earth, we are committing matricide. Even the images we use to sell things are indicative of the way we murder the feminine every day. Billboards show us larger-than-life photographs of emaciated women, women starving, women ravaged. Even the television shows we honor are all about triumph over the "other," cutting out opponents like we do trees. Reality television shows us that the name of the game is "Who will be the chosen one?" and "Who will win?" We pant for the next episode. We are being fed fast food at every corner by a collective patriarchal force that tells us to drive harder and faster, to become more perfect, skinnier, and richer or die. As if we aren't half dead already. This is why Saturn is the smelling salt that can wake us from our slumber and give us new rules to live by. Our structure, as evidenced by the current state of affairs, frankly sucks.

The crisis of faith that many of us endure is equal to the accelerating rate at which we continue to become disconnected from our inner guidance, images, and meaning by handing over our authority to external sources like celebrities and fancy toys. Like hungry lions, they lie in wait, ready to prey upon our weaknesses to feed their own. It's like the mugger who identifies his next victim by watching for an arrhythmic pattern in his or her walk to take advantage of that disconnectedness. Saturn is the part of us that connects us to the formidable strength at our core that can ward off external exploits that undermine our authority or just plain rip us off from our own resources.

We have become estranged from the subtler but sacred experiences that our souls need to feel alive. Our contemporary "supersize" mentality strips us of our creativity and soul food. We are getting too lazy, and we are often uninspired. We let our sitcoms, billboards, magazines, portable digital assistants, and pop-ups do the thinking for us. We're certainly not the first to lament over the demythologization and desacralization of our world. Yet, as dim as our pilot light might feel, it is waiting to burn with a fury if only we ignite this rich inner world of which the planets are an integral part. When we are truly in tune with the messages of our inner world, life can feel like a nonstop series of uncanny, serendipitous, and magic moments. We can experience this through the imagery in our dreams, meditation, self-reflection, psychotherapy sessions, communing with nature, or late-night existential musings with our closest confidante. When we reflect on the messages and synchronicity of those sorts of moments, we remain present and plugged into ourselves, and life becomes truly numinous. And Saturn is the anchor. Vedic scholar Robert Svoboda says, "If you can live your life in continual remembrance of Saturn's presence you will never need to mourn your fate, for you will have become truly conscious of the pervasiveness of the Realness of the Real."

Why Saturn Is the Metaphor for Our Time

Joseph Campbell, in his famous interview series with Bill Moyers right before Campbell's death, said: "I don't think what we're looking for is the meaning of life but a feeling of being alive!" Live fully and be ready to work out the karma thrown your way. This is one of Saturn's most important teachings. Life is getting down into the guts, the sewers, and the trenches to confront whatever keeps you weak and lifeless. Get to work because there is no time to waste. Since September 11, 2001, Saturn has been bellowing in all four corners of the American psyche: "Welcome to the rest of the world and wake up! Time is of the essence," he has been saying, "so give up your naive McDonaldland comfort zones and smell the damn coffee!" What are your priorities right now? (Let's not even talk about next week.) How many people quit their unfulfilling jobs, broke out of dead-end relationships, and withdrew their rainy-day savings after the sky fell in on that day? Saturn says that the rainy day is now. Where is our investment in that? We'll keep missing the boat if we think life is about something "later" or "over there." If we need the threat of "What future?" to wake us up, that's exactly what Saturn, as the world, is prepared give us.

Saturn, as the symbol of time, serves as the crucial link between our present reality and our potential reality. Through the limitations and the lessons that can be experienced only in the realm of time, we can work out our karma. All of the things in our lives that we feel unable to prevent are what we call fated. If you can't seem to meet anyone, or if you are endlessly mired in debt, or if you get sick, you usually believe that these things are beyond your control. Saturn is the teacher of humility, patience, and endurance. When you are in crisis, he is sending you a message. According to Svoboda, the best way to move through Saturn's "essence of misery" is to have faith and use your discrimination. When you're in the middle of any Saturn transition, the desire to heal has to be crucial, or the lesson probably won't break though.

Saturn is the referee of our lives. He keeps track of whether or not we are playing by the golden rules. He's not a moralist, although he's often accused of it. But he is that part of physics that says "every action has an equal and opposite reaction." In other words, it's not about judgment, it's about consequence. The rules do seem to change with the times, but the fundamental principles that keep track of the balance sheet remain.

If you really want to understand Saturn, look at the way you experience time. How have you chosen to spend the majority of it? Eating? Thinking about not eating as much? Sleeping? Drinking? Judging? What you worship is where your minutes go. Saturn is like your wireless phone company, keeping track of your minutes. Spend them wisely before you go over the limit. They are too expensive to waste.

"I Know You Are, but What Am I?"

Why are we still giving away our authority? We need the copyrights back to the scripts of our lives. We are letting the outside world devour us like a negative Saturn figure instead of trusting our own inner guru to make up the rules. Caroline Casey reminds us that whenever we encounter fear, difficulty, or depression we are meeting major red flags that tell us we have given our authority away whether to a lover, father, police officer, or boss. For women, the father sets the tone for how we will deal with authority and rules in general. How do we still seek our father's approval either consciously or unconsciously? Until we heal the brokenness of our Saturn placement, we continually meet people, particularly men, who dance with us in a grand unfolding of our early patterning. If our fathers failed us and reinforced Saturnian insecurities, we are likely to meet men who will push exactly the buttons to force us to face our demon. When we are unconscious and refuse to take on Saturn in the most active way, a parade of "he's" will come around and remind us what the lesson is. Once we get the lesson, no matter what our Saturn placement is, relationships to men in general are apt to be improved. We will stop turning to men for approval and begging them to tell us that yes, we are very good girls. Saturn insists that we learn to please ourselves first.

Keeping Track

The karmic boomerang always comes back. If we steal we might lose something ourselves or get robbed. Maybe not for twenty years, maybe not even in the next lifetime, but be assured that Saturn will keep track. In her commentary on the *Course in Miracles*, Marianne Williamson, self-help guru and lecturer, says that if you speak from your ego, the other person's ego will speak back to you. But if you speak from your heart, you will get a heartfelt response.

If we're not ready to face the assignment that Saturn has given us as our life teacher, we could end up engaging in relationships with those that allow us to hide out in denial. We sometimes want to surround ourselves with folks who will tell us we're precious little angels, to opt out of doing the painstaking work of making our own rules. Again, these are not one-sided moralistic judgments. It's just physics. We judge because we never have the full picture, the experience of walking in the other's shoes. Do we even know the whole of our own story?

Nothing Personal, Ma'am

Of course people like to project their own morality issues onto Saturn. Let's call this Saturn gone awry. This is how Saturn got the rep of being the bad guy. He's not religious, mind you. So we can't blame him for our legacies of Catholic or Jewish guilt, S&M tendencies, or "holier than thou" hypocrisy trips. He's not an evangelist. In other words, if we feel at the mercy of some "bad luck," it would be unfair to say that

Saturn hates us, believes we are possessed by evil, or believes that we are sinners. Saturn is not emotional or judging; human beings are. He's not trying to make us feel guilty or to get his way and lord power over us either. He just wants us to face the music and look at the consequences. If the shoe fits, he wants us to wear it. He doesn't care who designed it. In fact, he simply wants us be our own gurus and live by our own principles. The truth is that the only Bible-Belter you should pay heed to has to be the one inside your own soul. Don't be fooled into thinking that Saturn is that angel on your right and devil on your left shoulder. He is your life, the tablet you have been writing on since the beginning of time.

Seven-Year Itch

Saturn will test you at the following crucial ages: seven, fourteen, twenty-one, and of course, the momentous Saturn Return when you're about to turn thirty. At seven, you are fully ensconced in the school system in which you must learn social rules. Your personality is in development and social comparison truly begins. Any feelings of being different from your peers can be traumatic at this delicate young age. By age fourteen, childhood is ending and your confrontation with authority starts full force. Your relationship with parental figures is of primary issue and there tends to be rebellion, withdrawal, and limit testing. This is also a crucial stage, one in which you often experience alienation and confusion. The polarity between self and other is radical at this stage. It is common to experience states of longing, agonizing, and searching. We seek out and write poetry and look for philosophies that will offer us solace in our adolescent angst. We search for meaning and guidance like never before. With the lack of strong role models in the postmodern world, we look to our musicians and pop-culture icons. From twenty-one until the Saturn Return we encounter some of our most dynamic and experimental years. Some of us form families or finally leave the family of origin. It is said that many of us dance with death during this time or at least harbor fantasies that we will die young. For some it is impossible to imagine being alive after thirty. In any case, chaos is often rampant as all the loose ends start to unravel so that we may put them back together again, creating our own rules, and start over again at the Saturn Return.

Saturn Is Not the Enemy

How many of our friends and clients in the anguish of their lessons lament: "Saturn hates me!" This is not true. He is the ally, not the enemy. Our real purpose in writing this book is to get you to wrap your brain around this. But know that he is not the warm fuzzy friend that's going to sugarcoat and help you rationalize your bullshit. He's the tough-love taskmaster who came to raise the bar so you can grow up and keep growing. The other typical plea is: "Can't we just get rid of Saturn altogether?" Sure, no problem. Just imagine no more stop signs and everyone driving on whatever side of the road they feel like, your floor dropping out, no ceilings, no walls, no skin, no bones, no support. In reality, we could all use a little more Saturn, not less.

How many of us are living up to our true potential? Have you met *you* yet? What would you say if someone asked you what you are all about and probed deeper than a Barbara Walters interview? Would you exaggerate your persona, would you break down in tears, or would you know your truth and speak from your soul? Are you still trying to impress someone "out there"? Are you in the world but not *of* it? Or does the world weigh on your shoulders? No matter what Saturn lesson you are currently in, at the Return or otherwise, these questions need to stay alive if you are to stay on your game.

As we face ourselves, are we willing to slide all the way down the mountain and hike up the other side again? If we listen to Saturn, there is no need to experience Sisyphean struggles. The boulders you shoulder will get lighter and lighter. Instead of fighting Saturn, you have to learn to love him and to embrace the beauty of being an adult. There's no going back to childish things now. Saturn can liberate you from clinging to the toys you should have given up years ago. Turning thirty is a gift, because these can be the best years of your life.

Additional Reading

Campbell, Joseph. 1972. *The Hero with a Thousand Faces.* Princeton, NJ: Princeton University Press.

Estés, Clarissa Pinkola. 1992. *Women Who Run with the Wolves: Myths and Stories of the Wild Woman Archetype.* New York: Ballantine Books.

Greene, Liz. 1976. *Saturn: A New Look at an Old Devil.* New York: S. Weiser.

Jung, Carl. 1976. *Psychological Types.* Princeton, NJ: Princeton University Press.

Steinbrecher, Edwin. 1988. *The Inner Guide Meditation: A Spiritual Technology for the 21st Century.* York Beach, ME: S. Weiser.

Sullivan, Erin. 1991. *Saturn in Transit: Boundaries of Mind, Body and Soul.* New York: Arkana.

Svoboda, Robert. 1997. *The Greatness of Saturn: A Therapeutic Myth.* Albuquerque, NM: Sadhana Publications.

Woodman, Marion. 1992. *Leaving My Father's House: A Journey to Conscious Femininity.* New York: Random House.

————. 1985. *The Pregnant Virgin: A Process of Psychological Transformation*. Toronto: Inner City Books.

————. 1991. *The Ravaged Bridegroom*. Boston: Shambhala Publications.

Index

Addictions and substance abuse
    Cancer and, 82
    Capricorn and, 164, 175, 176
    Pisces and, 199, 202, 205, 208,
        209–10
    Virgo and, 106
Adler, Alfred, 4
Allen, Woody, 199
Amos, Tori, 182
Amritanandamayi, Mata, 4–5, 25, 41,
    206
Andrews, Julie, 108
Anima/animus, 120, 125
Aniston, Jennifer, 30
Anorexia, 44
Appearance
    Aries and, 30, 35–37, 39
    Virgo and, 105
Aquarius, 178–93
    analytical side of, 182–83
    defining qualities, 179
    eccentricity and, 184
    facing the Saturn Return, 188–90
    famous people in, 182
    father issues and, 187
    freaky side of, 180–81, 184–85, 193
    friendship and, 181, 182, 183, 184,
        188, 190–92, 193

goals of, 189–90
group activities and, 185, 189, 193
hopes and wishes of, 186, 189
loneliness and, 181, 182
potentials in Saturn Return, 193
real-world Saturn Return stories,
    190–92
rebelliousness of, 185
Saturn location chart, 20
scientific talent in, 186–87
social acceptance and, 180–81
social butterfly syndrome and, 182,
    188
social climbing by, 183–84
survival skills, 191
Aries, 24–39
    authority and, 29, 33, 39
    defensiveness of, 27
    defining qualities, 25
    facing Saturn Return, 33–34
    famous people in, 30
    father issues and, 32–33, 36
    internal conflicts of, 28, 30–31
    intimacy issues of, 31–32
    need to be first, 28
    physical activity and, 34, 39
    potentials in Saturn Return, 39
    power and, 29, 34, 37–39

About the Authors

Stefanie Iris Weiss, M.A., is a writer, professor of writing and gender studies, and professional astrologer. She is the author of five self-help books including, most recently, *Coping with the Beauty Myth: A Guide for Real Girls*. Her other books have covered topics as diverse as grief, yoga, and veganism. She has written about astrology since 1996 and was a senior contributor to *Your Birth Sign Through Time* as well as a contributor to *Love Signs and You*. Stefanie holds a master's degree in English education from New York University, and a B.A. in English and women's studies from New York University. She has taught at Mary-mount Manhattan College since 1998.

Sherene Schostak, M.A., is a Jungian psychotherapist and a professional astrologer in private practice in New York City. She is also the creator of *Zodiac Dance: The Work-Out* DVD and the workshops from which it was derived. She holds a master's degree from New York University in clinical psychology and completed advanced graduate work in psychoanalytic studies at the New School for Social Research. In addition, Sherene has had specialized training in working with addictions, having worked closely with recovery groups for five years as a senior research assistant for the National Drug Research Institute. She is certified by the D.O.M.E. Inner Guide Meditation Center as an inner guide meditation initiator. She teaches classes and workshops internationally on astrology, archetypal psychology, Eastern philosophy, and Middle Eastern dance.

Together, they run Saturn Return workshops for women and offer private, individualized Saturn Return readings. They are the official astrologers for *Teen Vogue*. For more information, visit their website at saturnreturn.net.

Stefanie Iris Weiss

Copyright © 2003 Ralf Nau

Sherene Schostak

Copyright © 2003 Charles Eshelman